best easy dayhikes
Northern Sierra

Ron Adkison

FALCON®

HELENA, MONTANA

A FALCON GUIDE®

Falcon® Publishing is continually expanding its list of recreational guidebooks. All books include detailed descriptions, accurate maps, and all information necessary for enjoyable trips. You can order extra copies of this book and get information and prices for other Falcon® books by writing Falcon, P.O. Box 1718, Helena, MT 59624, or calling toll free 1-800-582-2665. Also, please ask for a copy of our current catalog. Visit our website at www.FalconOutdoors.com or contact us by e-mail at falcon@falcon.com.

1 2 3 4 5 6 7 8 9 0 TP 04 03 02 01 00 99

Falcon and FalconGuide are registered trademarks of Falcon® Publishing, Inc.

Project Editor: Molly Jay
Production Editor: Larissa Berry
Copyeditor: Durrae Johanek
Page Compositor: BookSetters
Book Design by Falcon Publishing, Inc.

Cataloging-in-Publication Data is on file at the Library of Congress.

CAUTION

Outdoor recreational activities are by their very nature potentially hazardous. All participants in such activities must assume responsibility for their own actions and safety. The information contained in this guidebook cannot replace sound judgment and good decision-making skills, which help reduce exposure, nor does the scope of this book allow for the disclosure of all the potential hazards and risks involved in such activities.

Learn as much as possible about the outdoor recreational activities in which you participate, prepare for the unexpected, and be cautious. The reward will be a safer and more enjoyable experience.

 Text pages printed on recycled paper.

Contents

Introduction: What is a best easy day hike? v
Ranking the Hikes vii
Zero Impact viii
Make It a Safe Trip xi
The Silent Killer xv
Map Legend xvii

The Hikes
1. Silver Lake to Gold Lake 1
2. Smith Lake Trailhead to Long Lake 6
3. Smith Lake Trailhead to Smith Lake 11
4. Frazier Falls 13
5. Round Lake 16
6. Feather Falls National Recreation Trail 19
7. Grouse Ridge to Glacier Lake 25
8. Alpine Meadows Road to Five Lakes 31
9. Schneider Camp to Showers Lake 35
10. Carson Pass to Frog, Winnemucca,
    and Round Top lakes 39
11. Ebbetts Pass to Nobel Lake 45
12. Sardine Falls 49
13. St. Marys Pass 53
14. Blue Canyon 57
15. County Line Trailhead to the Dardanelles 63
16. Gianelli Trailhead to Powell Lake 67

17. Green Creek to Green Lake 73
18. Emma Lake 77
19. Saddlebag Lake to Greenstone Lake 83
20. Saddlebag Lake Road to Gardisky Lake 87

For More Information 91

About the Author 93

Introduction

For the purposes of this book, the halfway point of the Sierra Nevada separates the range into northern and southern halves, and Yosemite National Park is located at about that halfway point. More important, Yosemite represents a transition in the Sierra, from very high and extremely rugged mountains to a more subdued landscape, with generally lower elevations and a well-developed forest cover. The northernmost 12,000- and 13,000-foot peaks of the Sierra punctuate the Yosemite backcountry, and the park is dominated by the last great expanse of granite in the range, save for the Desolation Wilderness west of Lake Tahoe. This final stretch of terrain in the High Sierra is profound, for Yosemite harbors some of the biggest walls in the world, and certainly some of the most dramatic spires and domes in the Sierra.

The granitic rocks of the Sierra continue northward from Yosemite, but they are still buried beneath ancient layers of volcanic rocks. Thus, the landscape of the Northern High Sierra is dominated by volcanic peaks. From Lake Tahoe northward to the terminus of the Sierra near Lake Almanor, the volcanics gradually diminish and granite once again dominates the landscape.

The high country of the Sierra becomes gradually more narrow and the elevations lower as you travel north from Yosemite toward Lake Tahoe. Farther north, only isolated pockets of moderately high, subalpine terrain punctuate the Sierra crest.

Although the Northern Sierra doesn't contain the vast contiguous wilderness the Southern Sierra does, this region still claims more than 1.2 million acres of roadless backcountry in eight wilderness areas, plus several other areas managed as roadless or as potential wilderness additions. Eight highways cross the Sierra Nevada crest between Yosemite and Lake Almanor, and though these roads sever many of the Northern Sierra's wild areas, they do provide excellent access to the forested west slope, to the high country, and to the drier east side of the range. What's more, many of these highways are kept open during winter, affording access to the high country for cross-country skiers and snowshoers.

The size of the Northern Sierra's wild areas, combined with the easy access, makes backcountry trips here suitable not only for extended backpacks but for weekend and easy day hiking trips as well. Except for the Lake Tahoe region and parts of Yosemite, hikers will find much of the Northern Sierra to be surprisingly uncrowded.

There are far more easy day hikes in the Northern Sierra than this little book might suggest, yet few hikers would argue that the 20 short hikes described here are not among the best short day hikes north of Yosemite.

Ranking the Hikes

Easiest   Frazier Falls
Saddlebag Lake to Greenstone Lake
Round Lake
Sardine Falls
Smith Lake Trailhead to Smith Lake
Silver Lake to Gold Lake
County Line Trailhead to the Dardanelles
Carson Pass to Frog, Winnemucca, and Round
Top lakes
Smith Lake Trailhead to Long Lake
Gianelli Trailhead to Powell Lake
Green Creek to Green Lake
Ebbetts Pass to Nobel Lake
Feather Falls National Recreation Trail
Grouse Ridge to Glacier Lake
Alpine Meadows Road to Five Lakes
Schneider Camp to Showers Lake
Blue Canyon
Emma Lake
Saddlebag Lake Road to Gardisky Lake
Hardest   St. Marys Pass

Zero Impact

Going into a wild area is like visiting a famous museum. You obviously do not want to leave your mark on an art treasure in the museum. If everybody going through the museum left one little mark, the piece of art would be quickly destroyed—and of what value is a big building full of trashed art? The same goes for pristine wildlands. If we all left just one little mark on the landscape, the backcountry would soon be spoiled.

A wilderness can accommodate human use as long as everybody behaves. But a few thoughtless or uninformed visitors can ruin it for everybody who follows. All backcountry users have a responsibility to know and follow the rules of no-trace camping.

Nowadays most wilderness users want to walk softly, but some aren't aware that they have poor manners. Often their actions are dictated by the outdated habits of a generation of campers who cut green boughs for evening shelters, built campfires with fire rings, and dug trenches around tents. In the 1950s, these "camping rules" may have been acceptable, but they leave long-lasting scars, and today such behavior is absolutely unacceptable. Wild places are becoming rare, and the number of users is mushrooming. More and more camping areas show unsightly signs of heavy use.

Consequently, a new code of ethics is growing out of the necessity of coping with the unending waves of people who want a perfect backcountry experience. Today we all must leave no clues that we were there. Enjoy the wild, but leave no trace of your visit.

Three Falcon Zero-Impact Principles

- *Leave with everything you brought in.*
- *Leave no sign of your visit.*
- *Leave the landscape as you found it.*

Most of us know better than to litter—in or out of the backcountry. Be sure you leave nothing, regardless how small it is, along the trail or at your campsite. This means you should pack out everything, including orange peels, flip tops, cigarette butts, and gum wrappers. Also, pick up any trash that others leave behind.

Follow the main trail. Avoid cutting switchbacks and walking on vegetation beside the trail. Don't pick up "souvenirs," such as rocks, antlers, or wildflowers. The next person wants to see them too, and collecting such mementos violates many regulations.

Avoid making loud noises on the trail (unless you are in bear country) or in camp. Be courteous— remember, sound travels easily in the backcountry, especially across water.

Carry a lightweight trowel to bury human waste 6 to 8 inches deep and at least 300 feet from any water source. Pack out used toilet paper. Keep human waste at least 300 feet from any water source.

Finally, and perhaps most important, strictly follow the pack-in/pack-out rule. If you carry something into the backcountry, consume it or carry it out.

Leave no trace—and put your ear to the ground and listen carefully. Thousands of people coming behind you are thanking you for your courtesy and good sense.

Details on these guidelines and recommendations of Zero Impact principles for specific outdoor activities can be found in the FalconGuide *Leave No Trace*. Visit your local bookstore or call Falcon Publishing at (800) 582-2665 for a copy.

Make It a Safe Trip

The Boy Scouts of America have been guided for decades by what is perhaps the single best piece of safety advice— Be Prepared! For starters, this means carrying survival and first-aid materials, proper clothing, compass, and topographic map—and knowing how to use them.

Perhaps the second-best piece of safety advice is to tell somebody where you're going and when you plan to return. Pilots must file flight plans before every trip, and anybody venturing into a blank spot on the map should do the same. File your "flight plan" with a friend or relative before taking off.

Physical conditioning is also important. Being fit not only makes wilderness travel more fun, it also makes it safer. For more knowledge of wilderness safety and preparedness, here are a few more tips.

- Check the weather forecast. Be careful not to get caught at high altitude by a bad storm or along a stream in a flash flood. Watch cloud formations closely so you don't get stranded on a ridgeline during a lightning storm. Avoid traveling during prolonged periods of cold weather.

- Avoid traveling alone in the wilderness.

- Keep your party together.

- Study basic survival and first aid before leaving home.

- Don't eat wild plants unless you have positively identified them.

- Before you leave for the trailhead, find out as much as you can about the route, especially the potential hazards.

- Don't exhaust yourself or other members of your party by traveling too far or too fast. Let the slowest person set the pace.

- Don't wait until you're confused to look at your maps. Follow them as you go along, from the moment you start moving up the trail, so you have a continual fix on your location.

- If you get lost, don't panic. Sit down and relax for a few minutes while you carefully check your topo map and take a compass reading. Confidently plan your next move. It's often smart to retrace your steps until you find familiar ground, even if you think it might lengthen your trip. Lots of people get temporarily lost in the wilderness and survive—usually by calmly and rationally dealing with the situation.

- Stay clear of all wild animals.

- Take a first-aid kit that includes, at a minimum, a sewing needle, snakebite kit, aspirin, antibacterial ointment, two antiseptic swabs, two butterfly bandages, adhesive tape, four adhesive strips, four gauze pads, two triangular bandages, two inflatable splints, Moleskin or Second Skin for blisters, one roll 3-inch gauze, CPR shield, rubber gloves, and lightweight first-aid instructions.

- Take a survival kit that includes a compass, whistle, matches in a waterproof container, cigarette lighter, candle, signal mirror, flashlight, fire starter, aluminum foil, water purification tablets, space blanket, and flare.

Last but not least, don't forget that the best defense against unexpected hazards is knowledge. Read up on the latest in wilderness safety information in the recently published *Wild Country Companion*. Check the back of this guidebook for ordering information.

You Might Never Know What Hit You

Mountains are prone to sudden thunderstorms. If you get caught by a lightning storm, take special precautions. Remember:

- Lightning can travel far ahead of the storm, so be sure to take cover before the storm hits.

- Don't try to make it back to your vehicle. It isn't worth the risk. Instead, seek shelter even if it's only a short way back to the trailhead. Lightning storms usually don't last long, and from a safe vantage point, you might enjoy the sights and sounds.

- Be especially careful not to get caught on a mountaintop or exposed ridge; under large, solitary trees; in the open; or near standing water.

- Seek shelter in a low-lying area, ideally in a dense stand of small, uniformly sized trees.

- Stay away from anything that might attract lightning, such as metal tent poles, graphite fishing rods, or pack frames.

- Get in a crouch position and place both feet firmly on the ground.
- If you have a pack (without a metal frame) or a sleeping pad with you, put your feet on it for extra insulation against shock.
- Don't walk or huddle together. Instead, stay 50 feet apart, so if somebody gets hit by lightning, others in your party can give first aid.
- If you're in a tent, stay there, in your sleeping bag with your feet on your sleeping pad.

The Silent Killer

Be aware of the danger of hypothermia—a condition in which the body's internal temperature drops below normal. It can lead to mental and physical collapse and death.

Hypothermia is caused by exposure to cold and is aggravated by wetness, wind, and exhaustion. The moment you begin to lose heat faster than your body produces it, you're suffering from exposure. Your body starts involuntary exercise, such as shivering, to stay warm and makes adjustments to preserve normal temperature in vital organs, restricting blood flow in the extremities. Both responses drain your energy reserves. The only way to stop the drain is to reduce the degree of exposure.

With full-blown hypothermia, as energy reserves are exhausted cold reaches the brain, depriving you of good judgment and reasoning power. You aren't aware that this is happening. You lose control of your hands and your internal temperature slides downward. Without treatment, this leads to stupor, collapse, and death.

To defend against hypothermia, stay dry. When clothes get wet, they lose about 90 percent of their insulating value. Wool loses relatively less heat than cotton, down, and some synthetics. Choose rain clothes that cover the head, neck, body, and legs and provide good protection against wind-driven rain. Most hypothermia cases develop in air temperatures between 30 and 50 degrees F, but hypothermia can develop in warmer temperatures.

If your party is exposed to wind, cold, and wet, think

hypothermia. Watch yourself and others for these symptoms: uncontrollable fits of shivering; vague, slow, slurred speech; memory lapses; incoherence; immobile, fumbling hands; frequent stumbling or a lurching gait; drowsiness (to sleep is to die); apparent exhaustion; and inability to get up after a rest. When a member of your party has hypothermia, he or she may deny any problem. Believe the symptoms, not the victim. Even mild symptoms demand treatment, as follows:

- Get the victim out of the wind and rain.

- Strip off all wet clothes.

- If the victim is only mildly impaired, administer warm drinks. Then get the victim in warm clothes and a warm sleeping bag. Place well-wrapped water bottles filled with heated water close to the victim.

- If the victim is badly impaired, attempt to keep him or her awake. Put the victim in a sleeping bag with another person—both naked. If you have a double bag, put two warm people in with the victim.

Map Legend

Interstate	🛣		Picnic Area	🪑
U.S. Highway	🛣 🛣		Campground	▲
State or County Road	🛣 🛣		Cabins/Buildings	■
Interstate Highway	⟹		Elevation	X 9,782 ft.
Paved Road	⟹		Peak	🏔
Unpaved Road, Graded	⟹			
Unpaved Road, Poor	=====⟹		Falls	⌇
Trailhead	○		Lake	🝆
Main Trail	～⌁⌁⌁		Pass/Saddle	)(
Secondary Trail	～⌁⌁⌁			
River/Creek, Perennial	～～		Map Orientation	
Spring	⌀			N ⬆
Forest/Wilderness/ Park Boundary	⌐⌐⌐～		Scale	

Map Orientation

N
△

Scale

0   30   60
Miles

1
SILVER LAKE TO GOLD LAKE

Highlights: This short, scenic hike leads to an ice-sculpted lake basin at the far northern end of the Sierra.

General location: Bucks Lake Wilderness (Plumas National Forest), 10 miles west of Quincy, and 35 miles northeast of Chico.

Distance: 3 miles.

Elevation gain and loss: +300 feet, -150 feet.

Trailhead elevation: 5,800 feet.

High point: 6,100 feet.

Best season: July through September.

Water availability: At Gold Lake; treat before drinking or bring your own.

Maps: Plumas National Forest map; Bucks Lake Wilderness map (topographic); USGS Bucks Lake 7.5-minute quad.

Permits: Not required.

Key points:

0.0 Silver Lake Trailhead; proceed southeast across the dam.

1.0 Junction with Granite Gap Trail; stay left (south).

1.5 Gold Lake.

Finding the trailhead: From California Highway 70/89 in Quincy, turn west onto the two-lane pavement of Forest Road 119, prominently signed for Meadow Valley and Bucks Lake. After 8.5 miles, turn right (northwest) onto FR 24N29X, signed for Silver Lake. This rough gravel road with frequent washboards is narrow and winding, steep in places, and quite rocky over the final 3 miles.

Follow this road for 6 miles, then turn left into Silver Lake Campground. The confined trailhead parking area is located at the road's end, on the northeast shore of Silver Lake next to the dam. If the trailhead parking area is full, as it often is on summer weekends, park at the campground entrance and walk 0.4 mile to the trailhead.

The hike: This rewarding, easy, short hike leads you through one of the northernmost lake basins in the Sierra Nevada. The Silver Lake cirque is a broad, mile-wide, ice-sculpted bowl spread out below Spanish Peak and the Sierra crest. The cirque contains numerous small lakes and tarns and is dominated by an expanse of glacier-polished bedrock.

The trail from Silver Lake to Gold Lake is well worn and easy to follow, with only a few moderately steep grades. Vistas are panoramic for much of the way to deep Gold Lake, which offers fair fishing and cool, late summer swimming. Nearby Rock Lake, a small rockbound tarn, offers better diving from its rocky shores, but the trail to it is much more rigorous than the easy trail to Gold Lake.

From the road's end at Silver Lake, the trail follows the Silver Lake dam, where you enjoy excellent views into the ice-sculpted cirque above. After leaving the dam, the signed Gold Lake Trail branches left away from the shoreline fishing access trail. Quickly thereafter you reach the boundary of the Bucks Lake Wilderness and a trail register.

From there you begin a steep ascent up the rocky moraine, where only a few white firs and Jeffrey pines cast scant shade among the fields of manzanita and huckleberry oak. After two short but steep pitches you crest the huge moraine, where far-flung vistas reach northwest past Silver Lake to distant Lassen Peak, east to sprawling American Valley, and southeast past Spanish Peak to the bold crags of Sierra Buttes.

From there you begin a gentle traverse across the south slopes of the brushy moraine, studded with widely scattered white firs, and Jeffrey and sugar pines. Excellent views from the trail stretch across the basin to the broken north buttress of Spanish Peak. In the distant south and southeast rise the rounded, forested ridges of the Northern Sierra, and far below the trail lies the soggy spread of Jacks Meadow.

After 1 mile, just after leaving the moraine and bending south, you reach a junction indicated by a trailside post. The Granite Gap Trail turns southwest here, ascending very steeply past Mud and Rock lakes, 0.5 mile and 200 feet above, eventually leading to the Pacific Crest Trail. But you continue straight ahead (south) toward Gold Lake. The rocky trail follows an undulating course across the ice-gouged basin above the bog of Jacks Meadow. It is a scenic, rockbound landscape, studded with only a scattering of Jeffrey pines and white firs.

Eventually you will spy the cascading outlet stream of Gold Lake, then drop down to a crossing of the small stream draining Rock Lake, which is often dry by late summer. From here, ascend one final, short and steep pitch to the ridge overlooking Gold Lake, then descend steeply for several yards to the lakeshore.

Gold Lake is a very beautiful, deep, and round lake, fed by several streams cascading from the heights above. A broken headwall of ice-polished bedrock rises behind the lake to the flat, fir-fringed Sierra crest. The dark, metamorphic rock of the north buttress of Spanish Peak forms a dramatic backdrop to the lake. A scattering of brush and pines fringes the lakeshore, yet there is little level ground to accommodate backpackers. Mud Lake, along the Granite Gap Trail, offers the only suitable campsites for backpackers in the basin.

After enjoying beautiful Gold Lake, either backtrack to the trailhead or follow the Granite Gap Trail up to Mud and Rock lakes.

Silver Lake to Gold Lake

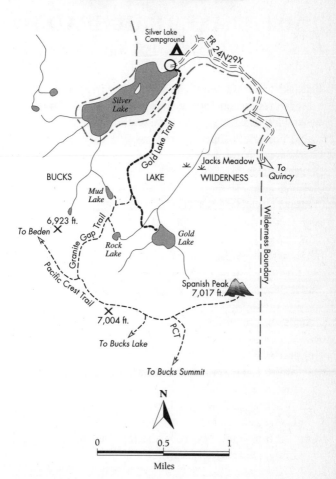

2
SMITH LAKE TRAILHEAD TO LONG LAKE

see map page 10

Highlights: This memorable, view-packed trip follows an un-crowded trail to one of the largest lakes in Lakes Basin.

General location: Lakes Basin Recreation Area (Plumas National Forest), 20 miles southeast of Quincy, and 35 miles northeast of Nevada City.

Distance: 4.8 miles.

Elevation gain: 750 feet.

Trailhead elevation: 5,800 feet.

High point: Long Lake, 6,546 feet.

Best season: July through September.

Water availability: At the lake. Treat before drinking, or bring your own.

Maps: Plumas National Forest map; USGS Gold Lake 7.5-minute quad.

Permits: Not required.

Key points:

0.0 Smith Lake Trailhead; follow the trail left (southwest) toward Long Lake.

0.25 Junction with unsigned, eastbound trail to Gray Eagle Lodge; stay right (south).

0.4 Junction with signed eastbound trail to Gray Eagle Lodge; bear right (south).

1.4 Junction with southeast-bound trail to Lakes Basin Campground; bear right (northwest).

2.4 Outlet of Long Lake.

Finding the trailhead: Follow California Highway 89 for 22.3 miles southeast from Quincy and 2.7 miles southeast from the CA 89/70 junction, or 47 miles northwest from Interstate 80 at Truckee, to the prominently signed turnoff to Lakes Basin Recreation Area. Proceed generally southwest on the two-lane pavement of Forest Road 24 for 5.2 miles to a prominently signed westbound spur road to Gray Eagle Lodge. This spur quickly sheds its pavement and becomes a rough gravel road. Cross a bridge spanning Gray Eagle Creek 0.3 mile from FR 24, then turn right onto a northbound spur road, signed for Smith Lake Trail and Gray Eagle Creek Trail at 0.4 mile. The trailhead is located at the loop at the road's end, 0.5 mile from FR 24. There you will find an information signboard with a map, and room to park 10 to 12 vehicles.

The hike: This memorable half-day hike leads through open forests and shady groves, passes rich wildflower gardens and ice-polished bedrock to one of the largest, and perhaps most beautiful, subalpine lakes in the Lakes Basin Recreation Area. With only occasional moderate grades, most hikers can reach Long Lake in about 1.5 hours via this gentle and uncrowded trail.

The trail begins at the west end of the loop at the road's end, adjacent to a signboard showing a map of Lakes Basin and listing various destinations and mileage. Turn left and proceed southwest toward Long Lake. Avoid taking the Smith Lake Trail, which branches right. Your trail proceeds through open Jeffrey pine forest and into a small bowl, where you step across the flow of a series of springs along the way. After 0.2 mile, ignore the eastbound trail leading to Gray Eagle Lodge, then briefly ascend to the top of a brushy moraine. After descending the south slopes of the moraine, you reach another eastbound trail at 0.4 mile, this one signed for the lodge.

Bear right (south) again, and follow the trail along the nearly level valley floor, staying a short distance west of Gray Eagle Creek, where you alternate between sunny openings and open forest, with abundant aspens along the nearby creek serenading you with the whisper of their fluttering leaves. The trail ahead soon passes into a moist, shady forest where the trail is decked with fern and dogwood, and after another 0.5 mile you reach the short left-branching spur trail to Hawley Falls along Gray Eagle Creek, a recommended side trip.

Beyond the trail to Hawley Falls, rise at a moderate grade to a signed junction at 6,150 feet, 1.4 miles from the trailhead. Turn left (northwest) at the junction, continuing a moderate ascent through the cool, shady forest. You will cross two channels of runoff draining the springs above, then ascend via switchbacks through a forest of pine, fir, and cedar. Bracken fern grows in profusion at the trailside.

The grade eases as you skirt the north and west shores of a lovely tarn fringed with grass and lodgepole pines. The gradual ascent ahead proceeds along the lake's cascading outlet stream, and you wind past an area of springs that nurture clumps of willows and an array of wildflowers, including leopard lily, cinquefoil, western wallflower, and meadow rue, as well as dogwood, serviceberry, and elderberry shrubs.

Huge erratic boulders and picturesque pines stud the rocky, ice-scoured landscape and signal your approach to the lake's outlet. The aptly named lake spreads out beneath the towering broken cliffs of Mount Elwell, with the ice-scoured cirque of Lakes Basin, studded with a discontinuous cover of conifers, rising behind the large lake to the Sierra crest. On a hot day it may be hard to resist a dip into the cool waters of the lake.

The trail continues along the rugged northwest shore of the lake but soon begins ascending talus slopes. The ice-polished bedrock around the lake's outlet affords the best diving and fishing access.

From the outlet area of beautiful Long Lake, hikers eventually retrace their steps to the trailhead.

Smith Lake Trailhead to Long Lake, Smith Lake, Frazier Falls, and Round Lake

To 89

Smith Creek

To 89

To 24

Smith Lake

Hike 3

Gray Eagle Creek

Grass Lake

Little Jamison Creek

Maiden Lake

Gray Eagle Lodge

Hike 2

24

Rock Lake

✕ 7,701 ft.

Frazier Creek

Wades Lake

✕

Jamison Lake

Mt. Elwell 7,812 ft.

✕

Long Lake

✕ 6,511 ft.

picnic area

Frazier Falls

Hike 4

To Pacific Crest Trail

Grass Lake

Lakes Basin Campground

Gold Lake Lodge

To Gold Lake Lodge

Big Bear Lake

Round Lake

Hike 5

7,550 ft. ✕

To Pacific Crest Trail

To 49

Gold Lake

N

0   0.5   1

Miles

LAKES BASIN RECREATION AREA

✕ 7,364 ft.

3
SMITH LAKE TRAILHEAD TO SMITH LAKE

Highlights: This fine short hike leads to one of the less-visited lakes in Lakes Basin, set in a cool forest of lodgepole pine beneath the north slopes of Mount Elwell.

General location: Lakes Basin Recreation Area (Plumas National Forest), 20 miles southeast of Quincy and 35 miles northeast of Nevada City.

Distance: 2 miles.

Elevation gain: 300 feet.

Trailhead elevation: 5,800 feet.

High point: Smith Lake, 6,094 feet.

Best season: July through September.

Water availability: Take your own.

Maps: Plumas National Forest map; USGS Gold Lake 7.5-minute quad.

Permits: Not required.

Key points:
0.0 Smith Lake Trailhead; follow the trail west, then north.
0.8 Junction with Mt. Elwell and Little Jamison Creek trails east of Smith Lake; turn right (west).
1.0 Smith Lake.

Finding the trailhead: Follow driving directions for Hike 2.

The hike: Most lakes in the Lakes Basin Recreation Area are rockbound, highly scenic, easy to reach, and, consequently, heavily visited. Smith Lake, in contrast, features no dramatic vistas and no rocky shore from which to dive or relax in the sun. What Smith Lake does offer is a peaceful destination about 30 minutes from the trailhead in a forested setting, far from the crowds that flock to other Lakes Basin waters.

The trail begins at the west end of the loop at the road's end, adjacent to a signboard showing a map of Lakes Basin and listing various destinations and mileage. From here, head north on the Smith Lake Trail. Your rocky trail ascends a moderate grade along the hot, brushy eastern slopes of Mt. Elwell's northeast ridge. Manzanita, huckleberry oak, and serviceberry mantle the slopes, with only a scattering of white fir and Jeffrey pine to cast small pockets of shade over the trail. Huge erratic boulders left behind as the last great glacier retreated into Lakes Basin, dot the slopes.

Eventually the trail curves around the ridge, then descends slightly into a cool mixed conifer forest, leading you to the grassy banks of the two small channels of Smith Creek. After a log crossing of the stream, a junction greets you on the west bank. Turn right onto the Little Jamison Creek Trail and stroll 0.2 mile to the limpid waters of lodgepole pine–fringed Smith Lake. The trail continues along the south shore of the lake before ascending to a saddle and then descends into the canyon of Little Jamison Creek.

Find a restful spot along the shore and enjoy the peaceful solitude of the easily accessible lake before backtracking to the trailhead.

4
FRAZIER FALLS

see map page 10

Highlights: This easy stroll quickly leads to a vigorous 176-foot waterfall in a scenic ice-sculpted landscape of the Northern Sierra.

General location: Lakes Basin Recreation Area (Plumas National Forest), 20 miles southeast of Quincy, and 35 miles northeast of Nevada City.

Distance: 1 mile.

Elevation gain: Negligible.

Trailhead elevation: 6,250 feet.

Best season: Mid-June through September.

Water availability: Take your own.

Maps: Plumas National Forest map; USGS Gold Lake 7.5-minute quad.

Permits: Not required.

Key points:

0.0 Frazier Falls Trailhead and picnic area.

0.3 Bridge Frazier Creek.

0.5 Frazier Falls overlook.

Finding the trailhead: Follow driving directions for Hike 2 to find Forest Road 24 leading from California Highway 89 to Lakes Basin Recreation Area and turn west. After 1.7 miles turn left (south) where a sign reads "Frazier Falls-4," and follow the paved one-lane road south. This is a narrow, winding, steadily ascending road with occasional turnouts; proceed with caution.

After driving 4.2 miles from FR 24, you will reach the Frazier Falls Trailhead, where there is ample parking on either side of the road and a picnic area with tables and pit toilets.

The hike: The Lakes Basin Recreation Area, an ice-sculpted landscape in the far Northern Sierra, offers a wide variety of rewarding recreational opportunities, ranging from scenic driving to boating, swimming, fishing, short walks to myriad lakes, and all-day hikes that survey the spectrum of the basin's landscapes. The short walk to impressive Frazier Falls is one of the best easy hikes in Lakes Basin and it follows the only trail in the basin that doesn't lead to a lake. The best time to take this hike is during peak snowmelt runoff, usually during May and June. Later in the summer the falls are but a trickle, yet the overlook at the trail's end still provides outstanding views of the narrow gorge of Frazier Creek.

The trail begins at the picnic site, and is well worn and easy to follow as it traverses a series of small benches between outcrops of gray ice-polished bedrock. Clumps of huckleberry oak are massed at the trailside between bedrock outcrops, and a scattering of lodgepole and Jeffrey pine, white fir, and juniper casts a modicum of shade.

After 0.25 mile of easy walking, you reach the wooden bridge spanning clear Frazier Creek, its banks fringed with dogwood and white-boled aspens. The trail briefly climbs above the course of the creek then turns away to gently ascend to an open, brushy ridge. From here, views open up, reaching across a tributary canyon to the glacier-sculpted slopes of Mills Peak, featuring broken cliffs, rocky chutes, brushfields, and cool groves of fir on its flanks.

From the ridge you wind your way over rocky terrain to the fenced-in overlook 0.5 mile from the trailhead. Your view of Frazier Falls and Frazier Creek's narrow, exciting gorge is unobstructed. A sign here indicates the falls begin at an elevation of 6,000 feet, 1.9 miles below Gold Lake, with a cascade of 248 feet, dropping a total of 176 feet. Tall firs in the canyon below and pines on the rim above allow you to judge the scale of the powerful falls and cascades. The falls surge over the brink of the bench above, then plummet down the narrow chute the creek has carved.

Good views reach down Frazier Creek canyon to distant mountains of the Eastern Sierra beyond. It is not hard to visualize this canyon full of glacial ice, as it was 10,000 years ago. The Frazier Creek glacier was hundreds of feet thick, illustrated by the ice-polished bedrock on the ridges far above the viewpoint.

After enjoying Frazier Falls, retrace your steps back to the trailhead.

5
ROUND LAKE

see map page 10

Highlights: This excellent short hike is a fine introduction to one of the northernmost glacial lake basins in the Sierra Nevada, and features good lake fishing and refreshing late season swimming.

General location: Lakes Basin Recreation Area (Plumas National Forest), 22 miles southeast of Quincy, and 35 miles northeast of Grass Valley.

Distance: 4.2 miles.

Elevation gain and loss: +200 feet, -80 feet.

Trailhead elevation: 6,600 feet.

High point: 6,800 feet.

Best season: July through early October.

Water availability: Take your own.

Maps: Plumas National Forest map; USGS Gold Lake 7.5-minute quad.

Permits: Not required.

Key points:

0.0 Trailhead at Gold Lake Lodge; proceed southwest on the doubletrack.

0.2 Trail to Big Bear Lake joins on the right; stay left on the doubletrack (southwest).

2.0 Junction with right-branching (northbound) trail to Round Lake; turn right (north).

2.2 Outlet of Round Lake.

Finding the trailhead: Follow California Highway 89 for 22.3
miles southeast of Quincy and 2.7 miles southeast of the
CA 89/70 junction, or 47 miles northwest from Interstate
80 at Truckee, to the prominently signed turnoff to Lakes
Basin Recreation Area. Proceed southwest on the two-lane
pavement of Forest Road 24. Follow this good paved road
south for about 7.5 miles.

Just before cresting a low summit on this road and before leaving Plumas County and entering Sierra County (at
the signed boundary), turn southwest onto an unsigned
paved road. Follow this road a very short distance to the
parking area opposite the access road to the Gold Lake
Lodge. A southbound road just beyond the parking area
leads to Gold Lake.

The hike: This hike through Lakes Basin, an area set aside for
day use only, surveys one of the northernmost glacial lake
basins in the Sierra Nevada. Ranging from lakeshores to windswept ridges with sweeping vistas, this trip allows you to experience the contrasting landscapes found in the far Northern Sierra. Fair fishing and cool swimming are always close at
hand in the basin, and easy side trips to numerous lakes are
made possible by the network of trails in the area.

From the parking area, proceed west toward a barrier
across a doubletrack and a sign showing a map of the area.
Begin hiking west along this doubletrack under a canopy of
red fir, passing outlying buildings of the Gold Lake Lodge
on your right.

After hiking 0.2 mile, you meet a northbound trail on
the right, leading to Big Bear Lake and beyond. Bearing

left here, proceed along the abandoned doubletrack through a forest dominated by red fir, at times passing grassy, wild-flower-speckled clearings. You sometimes have tree-framed views of Mount Elwell across the basin in the northwest, which, at 7,812 feet is the highest point in the Lakes Basin area.

Your route becomes increasingly rocky as you work your way up the basin and pass the old Round Lake Mine. Just beyond it is the right-branching trail leading down to Round Lake. Turn right (north) here and descend the doubletrack toward the aptly named lake. As you approach the lake the route narrows to singletrack, which leads you around the southeast shore of the lake toward the outlet, passing mine tailings and various detritus from the long-abandoned Round Lake Mine along the way.

This beautiful lake, resting at 6,714 feet, is backed up by a 750-foot headwall that rises southwest to the Sierra crest. Short and conical, snow-bent mountain hemlocks stud the broken rock of the headwall, and western white pine and red fir decorate the shoreline beneath rocky and brushy slopes. Fishing can be productive in the scenic lake, and a dip in its cool waters is sure to satisfy late-summer hikers.

From Round Lake, either retrace your steps for 2.2 miles to the trailhead or loop back to the trailhead via Silver, Cub, Little Bear, and Big Bear lakes, a hike of 2.1 miles.

6
FEATHER FALLS NATIONAL RECREATION TRAIL

Highlights: This pleasant hike through Northern Sierra foot-hills leads through pine and oak woodlands to the fourth highest waterfall in California.

General location: Feather Falls Scenic Area (Plumas National Forest), 15 miles northeast of Oroville.

Distance: 6.7 to 7 miles.

Elevation gain and loss: +500 feet, -1,000 feet.

Trailhead elevation and High point: 2,500 feet.

Low point: 1,600 feet.

Best season: March through November.

Water availability: Take your own.

Maps: Plumas National Forest map; USGS Brush Creek, and Forbestown 7.5-minute quads.

Permits: Not required.

Key points:

0.0 Feather Falls Trailhead.

1.3 Cross Frey Creek.

3.5 Feather Falls overlook.

Finding the trailhead: From California Highway 70 in Oroville, turn east onto Oroville Dam Boulevard (CA 162), and after 1.4 miles turn right onto Olive Highway. After driving 6.5 miles on this road, turn right onto Forbestown Road. A sign

Feather Falls National Recreation Trail

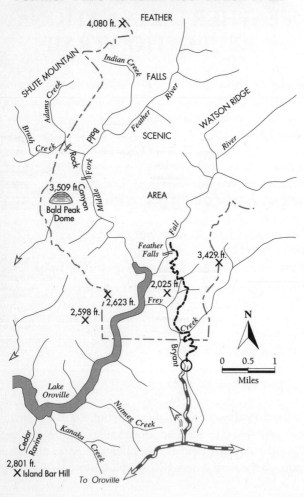

4,080 ft. X FEATHER

SHUTE MOUNTAIN

Indian Creek

FALLS

Adams Creek

Brush Creek

Bald Rock

Feather River

WATSON RIDGE

SCENIC

Middle Fork Canyon

River

3,509 ft.
Bald Peak Dome

AREA

Fall

Feather Falls

3,429 ft. X

2,025 ft. X

X 2,623 ft.

Frey

2,598 ft. X

Creek

Bryant

N

0   0.5   1
Miles

Lake Oroville

Nutmeg Creek

Kanaka Creek

Cedar Ravine

2,801 ft.
X Island Bar Hill

To Oroville

20

here points to Feather Falls. After another 6 miles turn left onto Lumpkin Road, where another sign indicates Feather Falls. After driving 10.8 miles on this paved but narrow and winding road, turn left just before reaching the small village of Feather Falls. A sign here indicates that the Feather Falls Trailhead is 2 miles north. After 0.2 mile of northbound travel, turn right and proceed 1.5 miles to the trailhead at the road's end where there is adequate parking space under the shadow of towering Douglas-fir and ponderosa pine. There is a developed campground here, with drinking water and toilets.

The hike: With a drop of 640 feet, Feather Falls is the fourth highest waterfall in California, and sixth highest in the contiguous United States. This foothills hike on the western slope of the Northern Sierra Nevada leads hikers through well-watered ponderosa pine forests and oak woodlands. The excellent trail maintains a gentle grade throughout. A new trail has been constructed here that follows a still more gentle approach to the falls, and you can follow both trails for a rewarding loop. Be aware that you may be sharing the trail not only with other hikers but mountain bikers and equestrians as well.

Your hike into the 15,000-acre Feather Falls Scenic Area begins at the information sign at the trailhead. Bear left at the junction with the loop trail and begin descending toward Frey Creek. The eastern segment of the loop follows a higher contour, losing 700 feet and gaining only 300 feet en route to the falls, and is best suited for the return trip to the trailhead.

Your trail leads north through an open forest of ponderosa pine and Douglas-fir, mixed with specimens of canyon live oak, black oak, and madrone. As you proceed along the gradually descending trail, you obtain occasional forest-framed views of the southeast face of Bald Rock Dome. Its sheer granite face rises impressively above Bald Rock Canyon on the Middle Fork Feather River and beckons adventurous climbers.

Among the trailside wildflowers that add their color to this foothills jaunt are Indian pink, yarrow, larkspur, and iris. The cool, shady forest of ponderosa pine, incense-cedar, Douglas-fir, and black oak reflects the 70 inches of average annual precipitation this relatively low-elevation area receives.

Take notice of the numerous patches of poison oak growing alongside the trail—the plant is unmistakable with its three-lobed, oaklike leaves.

As the trail makes its way into the Frey Creek environs, thimbleberry and bracken fern join the understory of this north-slope forest. Handrails along this switchbacking section remind you not to shortcut the trail.

Just beyond the 1-mile marker, the trail descends to the banks of Frey Creek, crossing above its boisterous waters via a wooden bridge. The trail then parallels the creek downstream above its east bank and, now on a southwest-facing slope, you will notice that canyon live oak begins to dominate the forest.

Soon, Bald Rock Dome comes into view again, and in spring, an impressive waterfall can be seen just north of the Dome.

As you continue descending high above noisy Frey Creek, you may notice the introduction of Indian paintbrush, monkey flower, and penstemon among the trailside flora.

After curving northeast, the trail descends into a shady Frey Creek tributary canyon where ponderosa pine and incense-cedar rejoin the forest. In moist areas such as this small canyon, large banana slugs, reaching lengths of 7 inches or more, can sometimes be seen making their way across the trail.

The trail crosses two small creeks, then ascends beneath a shady canopy of ponderosa pine, tanbark-oak, and black oak. Manzanita, lupine, and monkey flower constitute the understory.

The trail appears to be headed for a low, forested saddle on the northwestern skyline. As you ascend the last small gully toward that saddle, you may notice a few specimens of the seldom-seen California nutmeg. This interesting tree, sometimes confused with a fir, has sharply pointed, firlike needles.

Just before the trail attains the saddle, it veers eastward and begins traversing sunny, southeast-facing slopes. It switchbacks west on this open, live oak–clad hillside. The surrounding forest-covered mountains come into view and the trail becomes increasingly rocky.

A few digger pines (a California endemic) are seen just above, attesting to the hot, dry conditions that prevail on this sunny slope. The contrast between this slope and the forested slopes you just walked through provides a good example of the way slope aspect (the direction in which a slope faces) influences vegetation types at this low elevation.

Soon the trail bends northeast and, because of the precipitous nature of this rocky slope, is lined with handrails. You'll find the large Middle Fork Feather River and a major tributary, the Fall River, as you progress northeastward. You round a bend and are confronted with the awesome spectacle of roaring Feather Falls. This magnificent 640-foot falls plunge over a resistant granite precipice on its way to the Middle Fork Feather River and its impoundment in Lake Oroville. However, Feather Falls does tend to dry up considerably as the summer wears on.

Following the handrail-lined trail, turn left where a faint trail continues ascending along the course of Fall River, passing just above the brink of the falls. Here the upper segment of the loop joins on your right. Backpackers will want to continue upstream along the Fall River Trail for pleasant riverside campsites and good trout fishing.

After turning left, descend via one switchback and a wooden stairway to the fenced-in overlook platform precariously perched above the near-vertical gorge of the lower Fall River. This platform offers a head-on view of the impressive falls.

To the southwest you can see the upper end of the Middle Fork arm of Lake Oroville, 0.75 mile below. Adventurous boaters can view the falls from that point.

From Feather Falls, return to the trailhead the same way, follow the 3.2-mile upper segment of the loop trail, or ascend the Fall River Trail for about 2 miles to the trail's end.

7
GROUSE RIDGE TO GLACIER LAKE

Highlights: Typical of the far Northern Sierra, this trip provides ample rewards for minimal effort, following a good trail into a glacier-carved, lake-filled subalpine basin, and featuring far-ranging vistas, productive fishing, and refreshing late-season swimming.

General location: Tahoe National Forest, 22 miles west of Truckee, and 70 miles northeast of Sacramento.

Distance: 9.2 miles.

Elevation gain and loss: +650 feet, -600 feet.

Trailhead elevation: 7,500 feet.

High point: Glacier Lake, 7,550 feet.

Best season: July through early October.

Water availability: Take your own.

Maps: Tahoe National Forest map; USGS Graniteville, and English Mountain 7.5-minute quads.

Permits: Not required.

Key points:

0.0 Grouse Ridge Trailhead; proceed northeast on the trail.

0.1 Trail from campground joins on the right; continue straight ahead (northeast).

0.8 Junction with westbound trail to Milk and Island lakes; bear right (north).

1.7 Junction with northbound trail to Sawmill Lake; stay right (northeast).

Grouse Ridge to Glacier Lake

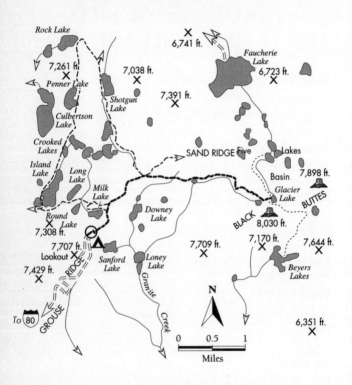

Rock Lake

7,261 ft.
×

Penner Lake

7,038 ft.
×

Shotgun
Lake

Culbertson
Lake

Crooked
Lakes

Island
Lake

Long
Lake

Milk
Lake

Round
Lake
7,308 ft.
×

7,707 ft.
×
Lookout ×

7,429 ft.
×

To 80

GROUSE RIDGE

Sanford
Lake

Downey
Lake

Loney
Lake

Granite Creek

6,741 ft.
×

Faucherie
Lake
6,723 ft.
×

7,391 ft.
×

SAND RIDGE Five Lakes

Basin
7,898 ft.
×

Glacier
Lake

BLACK BUTTES

8,030 ft.
×

7,709 ft.
×

7,170 ft.
×

7,644 ft.
×

Beyers
Lakes

6,351 ft.
×

N

0   0.5   1

Miles

26

1.8 Junction of Sand Ridge and Glacier Lake trails; bear right (east) onto Glacier Lake Trail.

4.6 Glacier Lake.

Finding the trailhead: From Interstate 80, 73 miles northeast of Sacramento, take the westbound California Highway 20 exit and proceed west for about 4.1 miles, then turn right (north) where a sign points to Bowman Lake. (This turnoff can also be reached by following CA 20 east from Marysville for 60 miles.)

Your road, Forest Road 18, has a good paved surface. As you proceed, follow signs at all junctions pointing to Grouse Ridge Lookout. After driving 6.2 miles from CA 20, turn right where a sign indicates that the Grouse Ridge Lookout is 6 miles ahead. On Forest Road 14 (dirt surfaced), proceed east, and after 1.3 miles bear right where a sign indicates Grouse Ridge Campground. After another 4 rough and dusty miles, bear left, passing the campground entrance, and follow signs pointing to Trail Parking Area. You will reach the parking area after another 0.2 mile, just beyond the left-branching spur road leading up to the Grouse Ridge Lookout.

The hike: An abundance of glaciated, subalpine scenery awaits hikers who complete this easy but moderately long hike to the Glacier Lake area. Side trips to Five Lakes Basin or Byers Lakes offer some cross-country challenge and a good chance for solitude.

From your ridgetop trailhead, you are treated to a superb sweeping panorama, encompassing the North Coast Ranges in the west, Lassen Peak in the northwest, the craggy

Sierra Buttes in the north, English Mountain in the northeast, Black Buttes in the east, and the peaks of the Granite Chief–Lake Tahoe region in the southeast.

Your route, closed to motorized vehicles, immediately begins descending northeastward through scattered western white pines. The trail from the campground quickly intersects your route on the right, and as you continue descending, red firs join the western white pines along this open ridge. Passing just east of Milk Lake amid thickening timber, you pass a westbound trail leading to Milk, Island, and Feeley lakes. Bearing right at the junction, continue wandering through the forest, now joined by an occasional lodgepole pine. In early summer, pine drops add a dash of red to the mostly lupine understory found along this forested stretch of trail. At times, spiraea is also a fairly common understory plant.

You soon pass a northbound trail leading to Sawmill Lake via the lake-filled basin to the north, and bear right onto Glacier Lake Trail. Avoid the Sand Ridge Trail ahead on your left, proceeding instead east through a small lodgepole pine–rimmed meadow. The somber Black Buttes loom on the skyline ahead.

Your gently ascending trail heads east through a meadow-floored forest of red fir and lodgepole and western white pine while passing rocky, glacially smoothed knolls at the foot of Sand Ridge.

En route you pass above a small lake that is in the advanced stages of transition from lake to meadow. Lodgepole pines, willows, and corn lilies are rapidly invading its shores.

Your route continues through lodgepole pine and red fir forest decorated by various wildflowers, and you steadily work your way toward the Black Buttes via increasingly rocky, glaciated terrain.

After hiking about 4 miles from the trailhead, the trail levels off on a subalpine flat before climbing briefly over an open rocky hill. From here you can gaze northeast to the rounded mass of 8,373-foot English Mountain, contrasting with the stark black crags of the Black Buttes to your immediate south. Snow patches cling to the Buttes long into summer.

Winding up and over another low hill, this one well forested, you reach Glacier Lake at 7,550 feet. This small but deep glacial tarn, set in a rockbound cirque at the very foot of the Black Buttes and fed by lingering snow patches, hosts a discontinuous forest of red fir, mountain hemlock, and western white pine above its rocky shores.

A few rewarding side trips are possible from Glacier Lake. For the average hiker, a 0.75-mile descent along Glacier Lake's outlet creek via a faint path provides access into the scenic, rockbound Five Lakes Basin.

For the more adventurous and experienced hiker, a southeastward ascent of 350 feet, over steep rock and grass slopes, above Glacier Lake to the obvious mountain hemlock–clad saddle on the skyline includes scaling, via Class 3 rock, the 8,030-foot-high point of Black Buttes. Otherwise, you can descend, first southeast, then southwest, for 1.25 miles from that saddle to remote Beyers Lake.

From Glacier Lake, return the way you came or turn north onto the Sawmill Lake Trail (1.7 miles from the trailhead), looping back via Penner, Crooked, Island, Long, Round, and Milk lakes for a grand tour of the area.

Alpine Meadows Road to Five Lakes

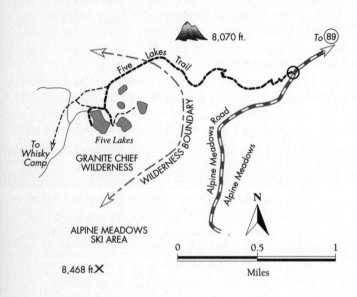

8,070 ft.

To (89)

Five Lakes Trail

WILDERNESS BOUNDARY

Five Lakes

To Whisky Camp

GRANITE CHIEF WILDERNESS

Alpine Meadows Road

Alpine Meadows

N

ALPINE MEADOWS SKI AREA

8,468 ft. X

| 0 | 0.5 | 1 |

Miles

8
ALPINE MEADOWS ROAD TO FIVE LAKES

Highlights: This short hike leads from one of Tahoe's famous ski resorts to an attractive timberline lake basin tucked beneath the Sierra crest.

General location: Granite Chief Wilderness (Tahoe National Forest), 5 miles west of Lake Tahoe and Tahoe City.

Distance: 3.8 miles or more.

Elevation gain: 1,000 feet.

Trailhead elevation: 6,560 feet.

High point: 7,550 feet.

Best season: July through September.

Water availability: At the lakes. Treat before drinking or take your own.

Maps: Tahoe National Forest map; USGS Tahoe City and Granite Chief 7.5-minute quads.

Permits: Not required.

Key points:

0.0 Alpine Meadows Road, Five Lakes Trailhead.

1.4 Granite Chief Wilderness boundary.

1.7 Junction with spur trail to Five Lakes; turn left (southwest).

1.9 Lower lake in Five Lakes basin.

Finding the trailhead: From California Highway 89, 3.8 miles northwest of Tahoe City, or 10 miles south of the West

Truckee exit off Interstate 80, turn west onto the prominently signed Alpine Meadows Road. Follow this paved two-lane road for 2.1 miles to the trailhead, indicated by a small destination and mileage sign on the right (north) side of the road. Park in turnouts here on either side of the road.

The hike: Resting atop the Sierra Nevada crest between the famous ski areas of Squaw Valley and Alpine Meadows, the shallow basin of Five Lakes sits in an easily accessible corner of the Granite Chief Wilderness. Although the trail gains 1,000 feet of elevation in about 2 miles, it is still a fairly easy and popular hike, yet usually not as crowded as are many trails in the Lake Tahoe area. Not only is the hike to Five Lakes a good leg stretcher, it also surveys contrasting landscapes, ranging from granitic bedrock to volcanic rocks and ski resorts to pristine wilderness. Swimming is a major attraction at the lakes, but the waters remain cold until late summer. The USDA Forest Service strongly discourages hikers from bringing dogs to Five Lakes, so heed the principles of Zero Impact and please leave your dog at home.

The inconspicuous signed trailhead is located on the north side of Alpine Meadows Road, where the trail begins next to a Granite Chief Wilderness information signboard. The trail immediately begins ascending a moderately steep grade upon steep slopes of brown volcanic rocks. Jeffrey pines offer occasional pockets of shade, but for the most part, you hike across sun-drenched slopes mantled in a blanket of manzanita, mountain whitethorn, and huckleberry oak.

During the first 0.5 mile, you will gain 300 feet of elevation at a steep grade; thereafter, the trail's grade moderates.

As you ascend, fine views open up into the broad volcanic bowl of the Alpine Meadows ski area, punctuated at its head by 8,637-foot Ward Peak. You will likely notice a number of granite boulders—erratics—strewn across the volcanic slopes. You will see the source of these boulders, after the grade abruptly moderates and you begin a long traverse. A large body of granite rises on the slopes of the Sierra crest ahead, the broken, ice-chiseled cliffs contrasting with the more subdued volcanic landscape in the nearby ski bowl.

After the trail levels out, the pine and fir forest thickens and casts more shade, but you continue across sunny openings filled with mule's ears and a variety of other summer blossoms. Soon you mount granite and begin to pass smooth, rounded outcrops and engage in a steady but moderate ascent via switchbacks. Jeffrey, western white, and lodgepole pines are much more widely scattered on these granitic slopes than on the richer volcanic soils below.

Traverse around the shoulder of a ridge at 1 mile, which affords more fine views and your last good look at Ward Peak and the ski bowl. The trail bends northwest, and you face only another 200 feet of climbing as you begin to traverse above a red fir–clad flat, gradually rising toward the small bowl above the flat. En route you pass an interesting dike of dark basalt, cutting through the granite toward the ridge above to the north. A pair of switchbacks leads across the dike, and from there you have a better view of the contrast between the dark volcanics and nearly white granite.

After approximately one hour of hiking, at 1.4 miles and 1,000 feet above the trailhead, you enter the Granite Chief

Wilderness at the head of a shallow basin in a cool stand of red fir. The trail is now nearly level and proceeds southwest through a forest of red fir, lodgepole, and western white pines, crossing a gentle, boulder-studded landscape. At 1.7 miles you reach the well-worn spur trail to Five Lakes at 7,560 feet. A sign here declares that no camping or stock is allowed within 600 feet of the lakes (at least 200 paces).

The westbound trail continues ahead for 0.5 mile to the Pacific Crest/Tahoe Rim Trail, and beyond for 2 miles to Whisky Creek Camp in the canyon far below. But you turn left onto the spur trail and quickly descend to the lowest and largest of the Five Lakes. There, various boot-worn trails branch left (southeast) to the upper lakes in the basin and lead partway around the lower lake.

The basin is a fine place for wandering and exploring, perhaps spending a few hours visiting all the lakes, swimming, or simply relaxing in the quiet beauty of the Northern Sierra. The gentle, granite-bound basin supports a timberline forest of mountain hemlock, western white pine, and red fir. Unfortunately, the chair lifts of Squaw Peak are painfully visible on the northern skyline.

After enjoying the Five Lakes basin, retrace your steps to the trailhead.

9

SCHNEIDER CAMP TO SHOWERS LAKE

Highlights: This view-packed timberline trip crosses the northern Sierra Nevada crest at the headwaters of the Upper Truckee River, where hikers enjoy panoramic vistas of the Lake Tahoe region, en route to scenic Showers Lake.

General location: Eldorado National Forest, 4 miles northwest of Carson Pass, and 13 miles southwest of South Lake Tahoe.

Distance: 4.4 miles.

Elevation gain and loss: +900 feet, -600 feet.

Trailhead elevation: 8,300 feet.

High point: 9,200 feet.

Best season: July through early October.

Water availability: At Showers Lake, 2.2 miles. Treat before drinking, or take your own.

Maps: Eldorado National Forest map, or Lake Tahoe Basin Management Unit map; Mokelumne Wilderness map (topographic); USGS Caples Lake 7.5-minute quad.

Permits: Not required.

Key points:
- 0.0 Schneider Camp Trailhead; proceed to the left (northeast) on the trail.
- 1.1 Reach Sierra crest at 9,200 feet and junction with eastbound trail descending Dixon Canyon; bear left (north) and begin descending.

Schneider Camp to Showers Lake

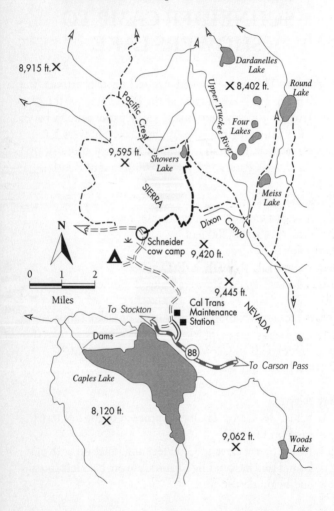

8,915 ft. ✗

Pacific Crest

Dardanelles Lake

✗ 8,402 ft.

Round Lake

Upper Truckee River

9,595 ft. ✗

Showers Lake

Four Lakes

SIERRA

Meiss Lake

Dixon Canyon

N

Schneider cow camp

✗ 9,420 ft.

0   1   2

Miles

✗ 9,445 ft.

To Stockton

Cal Trans Maintenance Station

NEVADA

Dams

88

To Carson Pass

Caples Lake

8,120 ft. ✗

9,062 ft. ✗

Woods Lake

2.2 Junction with Pacific Crest Trail (PCT) at Showers Lake.

Finding the trailhead: From California Highway 88 above the north shore of Caples Lake, about 102 miles east of Stockton and 3 miles west of Carson Pass, turn north where a sign indicates the CalTrans Caples Lake Maintenance Station. Drive past the maintenance station, and after 0.4 mile, turn right where a sign points to Schneider. The road becomes dirt at this point. Follow this occasionally rough and dusty road for 1.7 miles to the upper end of a broad meadow and park. The road continues on beyond a stock gate, but is a poor doubletrack.

The hike: Anyone who has hiked in the Lake Tahoe area knows how popular this region can be. In fact, some hiking areas in the region are downright overcrowded, and for good reason. The scenery here is often spectacular, and the hiking is generally easy.

This hike, traversing subalpine terrain for the entire distance, is by far the least-used trail in this area, save for the Showers Lake environs. Subalpine Showers Lake sees steady use, especially on summer weekends, but offers fine swimming and an exceptionally scenic setting.

From the east end of the large meadow known as Schneider Camp, your trail leads eastward past a sign indicating that the route is closed to motor vehicles. Pass through a stock gate and begin ascending volcanic slopes clothed in sagebrush and a variety of wildflowers.

As you near the top of your climb, you pass a few stunted whitebark pines, and after hiking 1.1 miles from the trailhead, you reach your high point atop the alpine Sierra Nevada crest. Vistas here are excellent. Below to the east lies the wide valley of the Upper Truckee River. Meiss Lake glistens in the middle of that subalpine valley and beyond are the southernmost summits of the Carson Range—Red Lake and Stevens peaks—both of which rise to 10,061 feet. Views also include the American River drainage in the west, the Freel Peak environs in the north, and the jagged peaks of the Ebbetts Pass region in the southeast, with higher peaks fading into the distance beyond.

Just after reaching your high point, you pass an east-bound trail descending Dixon Canyon and proceed north along the wildflower-clad east slopes of the Sierra Nevada crest. Quite soon, Round Lake and the Four Lakes come into view in the Upper Truckee River basin; beyond, Lake Tahoe begins to dominate your northward gaze.

Your briefly contouring trail now begins a descent toward Showers Lake, visible in a shallow basin in the north. After entering subalpine timber, your steep, gravelly route joins the Pacific Crest Trail (PCT) just before reaching Showers Lake. You turn left and begin skirting the numerous east shore campsites set amid a forest of mountain hemlock, red fir, and lodgepole and western white pines.

This fine lake is surrounded by glacially smoothed granite, lying just below the contact zone between the granitic rock and the volcanic material that buries the bedrock. Fishing here is poor, but the scenery is superb.

After enjoying Showers Lake and the Upper Truckee River valley, return the way you came.

10
CARSON PASS TO FROG, WINNEMUCCA, AND ROUND TOP LAKES

Highlights: This short but spectacular half-day hike leads to a trio of lovely timberline lakes near Carson Pass on the Sierra crest.

General location: Mokelumne Wilderness (Eldorado National Forest), 15 miles south of South Lake Tahoe, and 85 miles northeast of Stockton.

Distance: 6 miles.

Elevation gain: 730 feet.

Trailhead elevation: 8,573 feet.

High point: 9,440 feet.

Best season: Mid-July through September.

Water availability: At the lakes. Treat before drinking, or take your own.

Maps: Eldorado or Toiyabe national forest maps; Mokelumne Wilderness map (topographic); USGS Carson Pass, and Caples Lake 7.5-minute quads.

Permits: Not required for day hiking.

Key points:

0.0 Carson Pass–Pacific Crest Trail Trailhead

0.6 Junction with spur trail to Frog Lake; bear right (south).

0.7 Junction with eastbound Pacific Crest Trail; bear right (southwest) again.

Carson Pass to Frog, Winnemucca, and Round Top Lakes

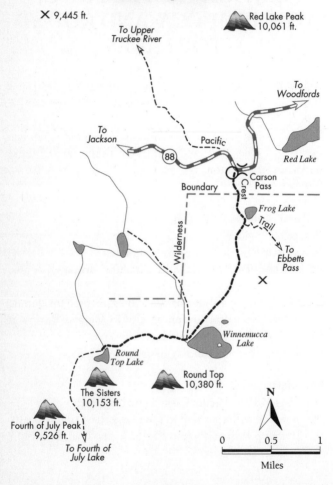

✕ 9,445 ft.

Red Lake Peak
10,061 ft.

To Upper
Truckee River

To Woodfords

To Jackson

Pacific

88

Red Lake

Carson
Pass

Boundary

Crest

Frog Lake

Trail

To Ebbetts
Pass

Wilderness

✕

Winnemucca
Lake

Round
Top Lake

Round Top
10,380 ft.

The Sisters
10,153 ft.

Fourth of July Peak
9,526 ft.

To Fourth of
July Lake

N

0   0.5   1

Miles

2.1 Outlet of Winnemucca Lake, and junction with trail descending northwest to Woods Lake; stay left (west) to reach Round Top Lake.

3.0 Round Top Lake.

Finding the trailhead: The spacious, but often-crowded, trailhead parking lot is located alongside California Highway 88 at Carson Pass, 8.8 miles southwest of the CA 88/89 junction, and 109 miles east of Stockton. A $3 self-issue parking fee is charged at the trailhead.

If the Carson Pass parking lot is full, which it often is during the summer, drive 0.25 mile northwest from the pass to the northbound Pacific Crest Trail Trailhead. A parking fee is also charged here.

Trailhead facilities include toilets, and interpretive and historical signs. Books, maps, and wilderness permits are available at the Carson Pass Information Station.

The hike: The hike to Frog, Winnemucca, and Round Top lakes is one of the most popular hikes in the Northern Sierra outside of the Lake Tahoe Area, and justifiably so. For a minimal investment of time and effort, you can enjoy some of the finest alpine scenery, broad vistas, and vivid wildflower displays along the northern crest of the range. As a result, you can expect to share the trail with many other hikers, but you probably won't notice them since your attention will be focused on the outstanding alpine scenery that lies just beyond the trailhead.

The trail, a combination of the Pacific Crest Trail, and part of the Winnemucca Lake Loop cross-country ski trail in winter, begins next to the Carson Pass Information Station, on the north side of the building. The trail mildly undulates at first, leading through an open forest of red fir, mountain hemlock, and lodgepole and western white pines, and crossing slopes of ice-polished granite bedrock. You will reach the signed Mokelumne Wilderness boundary, where the trail momentarily rises at a steep grade. Ahead, the grade moderates and leads gradually uphill all the way to Winnemucca Lake.

Beyond the wilderness boundary, lodgepole and whitebark pines dominate the open forest, and you wind among the trees and subalpine grasslands to the junction with the short spur trail to Frog Lake, just east of the main trail. Lodgepole and whitebark pines, and mountain hemlock stud the granite slopes around this beautiful, trout-filled lake, its waters lying in the foreground of a fine view northeast to the Freel Peaks and the Carson Range.

A brief ascent of several yards past Frog Lake leads to the junction with the eastbound Pacific Crest Trail, but you continue straight ahead, entering increasingly open slopes studded by a scattering of stunted pines. This openness affords tremendous vistas for every remaining step of the hike ahead.

The rubbly volcanic dome of Elephants Back rises above the trail to the southeast, a prominence seemingly more at home in the volcanic fields of the Nevada desert, rather than a feature of the Sierra crest. The towering broken crest of 10,380-foot Round Top, and the twin pyramids of the Sisters rise at the head of the basin in the southwest, their dark volcanic battlements contrasting with the light gray, bedrock below. Westward, you gaze out across Caples Lake and far down the west slope of the Sierra. Rising in the northwest are the distant high peaks of the Crystal Range in the Desolation Wilderness, and Red Lake Peak stands guard over Carson Pass in the north.

The trail ahead is gentle, with only occasional moderate grades. It is a classic walk through a High Sierra landscape, crossing slopes clad in willows and laced with early season rivulets, timberline meadows, and fields of vivid summer wildflowers. Among the myriad blooms, look for lupine, sulphur buckwheat, groundsel, alpine gold, paintbrush, western wallflower, whorled penstemon, Davidson's penstemon, mountain bluebells, blue flax, mule's ears, phlox, buttercup, red heather, and white heather.

After 1.9 miles, you crest a low moraine and stroll down to the shores of large and deep Winnemucca Lake, resting at an elevation of 9,000 feet. There are few places in the Sierra where such a timberline gem as this lake can be reached by such a short and easy hike. This kind of timberline landscape is reserved largely for backpackers deep in backcountry areas of the range. Only a scattering of stunted, tenacious whitebark pine and mountain hemlock clings to the granite shores of the round, island-studded lake. Bold volcanic cliffs rise 800 feet from the lakeshore, forming the dramatic headwall of the basin. Numerous creeks tumble and cascade into the lake from a lingering snowfield clinging to the walls above. Fishing for pan-sized brook, rainbow, and golden trout can be productive in the deep lake .

If you find Winnemucca Lake to be a bit too crowded, or if you simply want to stretch your legs some more, follow the westbound trail signed for Round Top Lake at the log crossing of Winnemucca Lake's outlet stream. This good trail ascends the west wall of the basin with occasional moderately steep grades. Round Top towers overhead while you cross alpine fell fields studded with wind-flagged whitebarks. After topping out on a 9,440-foot ridge among mats of krummholz, you gradually descend through fields of wildflowers and sagebrush to the willow-bordered shores of Round Top Lake at 9,300 feet.

With a backdrop of the somber volcanic cliffs of the Sisters, this beautiful heart-shaped lake hosts a timberline forest of whitebark pine around its shores that offer much more shelter than at windswept Winnemucca Lake. Fine views reach to the volcanic summits of Covered Wagon and Thimble peaks, and far to the Crystal Range in the north.

As you return to the trailhead, you will briefly spy a sliver of Lake Tahoe in the north as you cross the broad, open slopes just below Winnemucca Lake.

11

EBBETTS PASS TO NOBEL LAKE

Highlights: This short but scenic trip follows a segment of the Pacific Crest Trail that leads into a subalpine basin, set among volcanic peaks below the Sierra crest, near Ebbetts Pass.

General location: Toiyabe National Forest, 10 miles south-southwest of Markleeville, and 50 miles northeast of Angels Camp.

Distance: 7.4 miles.

Elevation gain and loss: +950 feet, -750 feet.

Trailhead elevation: 8,650 feet.

High point: Nobel Lake, 8,850 feet.

Best season: July through early October.

Water availability: Abundant at Nobel Lake. Treat before drinking, or take your own.

Maps: Toiyabe or Stanislaus National Forest maps; Carson-Iceberg Wilderness map (topographic); USGS Ebbetts Pass 7.5-minute quad.

Permits: Not required.

Key points:

0.0 Pacific Crest Trail Trailhead.

0.2 Junction with Pacific Crest Trail; turn left (east).

Ebbetts Pass to Nobel Lake

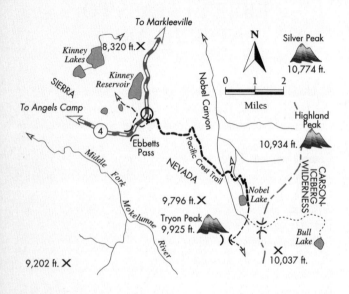

To Markleeville

Kinney Lakes

8,320 ft. ✕

Kinney Reservoir

SIERRA

To Angels Camp

Nobel Canyon

N

Silver Peak
10,774 ft.

0   1   2
Miles

Highland Peak

10,934 ft.

Pacific Crest Trail

4

Ebbetts Pass

NEVADA

9,796 ft. ✕

Tryon Peak
9,925 ft. ✕

Nobel Lake

CARSON-ICEBERG WILDERNESS

Bull Lake

✕ 10,037 ft.

Middle Fork

Mokelumne River

9,202 ft. ✕

2.5 Cross Nobel Creek.
2.7 Junction with northbound trail descending Nobel Canyon; stay right (south).
3.7 Nobel Lake.

Finding the trailhead: The signed Pacific Crest Trail Trailhead lies 0.1 mile east of California Highway 4, and about 0.4 mile north of Ebbetts Pass. This pass is 125 miles east of Stockton and 12.8 miles west of the CA 4/89 junction southeast of Markleeville.

The hike: This moderately easy hike uses a segment of the Pacific Crest Trail to reach the subalpine basin at the head of Nobel Canyon. From Nobel Lake you can scale Tryon Peak, hike southeast to remote Bull Lake, or just relax and enjoy the view and the magnificent surroundings.

The trail begins at the southwest (upper) end of the parking area, and proceeds south for 0.2 mile through a forest of lodgepole and western white pines, red fir, and mountain hemlock. Views through the trees across the highway to glacially smoothed granite and the volcanic pinnacles beyond help to make this stroll pass quickly.

Upon meeting the Pacific Crest Trail (PCT) you turn left, topping an open ridge at 8,800 feet, where you have good views north across the upper Silver Creek drainage. Then the trail contours through a timberline bowl under striking volcanic cliffs. You slice through a wildflower-dappled meadow, reenter a red fir, mountain hemlock, and western white pine forest, then contour around a granite spur ridge before beginning a side-hill descent. You have great views along this stretch across the deep, U-shaped trough of Nobel Canyon to 10,774-foot Silver Peak and 10,934-foot Highland Peak.

The gently descending trail leads southeast through a sparse boulder-dotted forest, crossing three small creeks en route. Just before reaching the bottom of Nobel Canyon, hop across two more small creeks, and notice that the granitic landscape you have been traversing changes into one dominated by volcanic material.

You then cross Nobel Creek and swing north briefly to round a spur ridge. The trail jogs south around that ridge, enters the shade of red fir and western white pine, then passes an unsigned trail on your left, descending the length of Nobel Canyon.

The trail contours into a gully containing Nobel Lake's outlet stream, and you then negotiate three long switchbacks while ascending a volcanic hillside, passing an occasional stunted juniper en route. Above this climb, you begin hiking along the outlet of Nobel Lake in increasingly alpine terrain dotted with a few stunted mountain hemlocks and whitebark pines, soon reaching the northeastern shore of Nobel Lake. This fine lake lies in a truly noble setting, surrounded by a grassy landscape decorated with a variety of wildflowers and scattered stands of whitebark pine and mountain hemlock, with a backdrop of craggy volcanic peaks. This lake can be a good producer of pan-sized golden trout.

From Nobel Lake, return the way you came.

12
SARDINE FALLS

Highlights: This easy, nearly flat hike leads to a foaming veil of whitewater in the volcanic high country east of Sonora Pass.
General location: Toiyabe National Forest, 1.5 miles southeast of Sonora Pass.
Distance: 2 miles.
Elevation gain: 200 feet.
Trailhead elevation: 8,800 feet.
High point: 9,000 feet.
Best season: Early July through September.
Water availability: Abundant; treat before drinking or take your own.
Maps: Toiyabe National Forest map; Hoover Wilderness map (topographic); USGS Pickel Meadow 7.5-minute quad.
Permits: Not required.

Key points:
0.0 Trailhead on California Highway 108.
1.0 Sardine Falls.

Finding the trailhead: There is no developed trailhead for this hike, only turnouts on either side of California Highway 108 on the northern margin of Sardine Meadow, and a "Route Closed to Motorcycles" sign on the south side of the highway. Find these turnouts by driving 2.5 miles southeast from Sonora Pass, or 12.2 miles west of the CA 108/

Sardine Falls

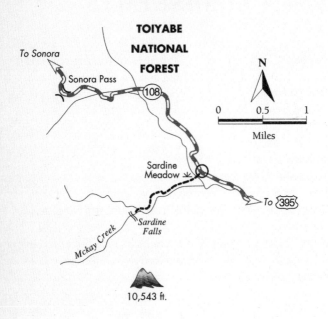

To Sonora

Sonora Pass

TOIYABE

NATIONAL

FOREST

108

N

0   0.5   1

Miles

Sardine
Meadow

To 395

McKay Creek

Sardine
Falls

10,543 ft.

U.S. Highway 395 junction, and 1.1 miles west of the signed Soda Creek bridge.

The hike: Anyone who has followed California Highway 108 over Sonora Pass knows how beautiful the volcanic landscape of the northern Sierra crest is in this area. The short hike to Sardine Falls near Sonora Pass is one of the best ways to enjoy this dramatic landscape without strapping on a backpack and committing to several long days on the trail. Even though the trail is obscured by cattle trails at the start, it is well defined thereafter, and is flat and easy enough for anyone who enjoys walking in the mountains.

Begin this hike on the south side of the highway, and proceed south past the "Route Closed to Motorcycles" sign and into the sagebrush-studded expanse of Sardine Meadow. The large veil of whitewater that is Sardine Falls plunges out of an alpine basin about a mile ahead, encircled by 10,000- and 11,000-foot volcanic peaks.

After about 150 yards, you will have to cross the shallow channels of Sardine Creek. This stream is usually less than ankle deep after August, so you may still get your feet wet. Thereafter, a well-worn trail, maintained by the cattle that graze the meadow in summer, leads into an open lodgepole pine forest alongside willow-bordered McKay Creek. Once you enter that forest your route follows the doubletrack of a long-closed road, with lupine and scarlet gilia growing in profusion along the trailside.

Whitebark pine joins the ranks of the forest, and after about 0.4 mile the creek ahead is funneled into a narrow gorge. Here the trail narrows into singletrack and ascends steeply, but briefly (the only steep grade on the hike), to a low ridge. Ahead the trail descends slightly southwest into a small meadow rich with willows and aspens, and the blooms of aster, corn lily, meadow rue, tall mountain helenium, cinquefoil, and paintbrush.

In the meadow the trail forks. Be sure to take the briefly rutted and sometimes muddy and overgrown right fork. Step across a small creek coming from the west, then follow a winding course into a broad open bowl with stark volcanic peaks rising above, their slopes feathered with tenacious whitebark pine.

As you approach the falls, you must rock-hop one last shallow stream, after which a number of boot-worn trails lead the final several yards to the base of the falls, a thundering 50-foot veil of whitewater plunging over a resistant cliff of gray volcanic rock. A scattering of lodgepole and whitebark pines offers convenient shade for viewing the falls. On a bench just below the falls, on the east side of the creek, you find several excellent campsites set in a grove of lodgepole pines.

From Sardine Falls, retrace your route to the trailhead.

13
ST. MARYS PASS

Highlights: This memorable hike quickly leads to an alpine Sierra ridge where far-ranging vistas of awe-inspiring mountain and desert scenery unfold.

General location: Stanislaus National Forest, 1.5 miles north of Sonora Pass, 45 miles northeast of Sonora, and 22 miles northwest of Bridgeport.

Distance: 2.5 miles.

Elevation gain: 950 feet.

Trailhead elevation: 9,450 feet.

High point: St. Marys Pass, 10,400 feet.

Best season: July through early October.

Water availability: None available. Take your own.

Maps: Stanislaus National Forest map; Carson-Iceberg Wilderness map (topographic); USGS Sonora Pass 7.5-minute quad.

Permits: A wilderness permit is required, and can be obtained at the Summit Ranger Station at the Pinecrest Lake turnoff on California Highway 108, about 30 miles east of Sonora.

Key points:
0.0 St. Marys Pass Trailhead.
1.25 St. Marys Pass.

Finding the trailhead: The trailhead lies at the end of a spur road, signed for Saint Marys Pass Trailhead, that leads north

St. Marys Pass

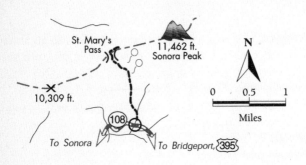

St. Mary's
Pass

11,462 ft.
Sonora Peak

10,309 ft.

108

N

0   0.5   1

Miles

To Sonora

To Bridgeport, 395

from California Highway 108 for about 100 yards. You will find this spur road about 0.8 mile west of Sonora Pass. The pass is 72.5 miles east of Sonora via CA 108, and 7.75 miles east of the Kennedy Meadows turnoff.

The hike: St. Marys Pass, high on the west ridge of Sonora Peak, offers rewards of far-flung vistas of the Central and Northern Sierra Nevada, making this short trip one of the best easy day hikes anywhere along the Sierra Nevada crest. Although the closed road and trail that lead to the pass are moderately steep in places, most hikers can reach the pass in about 30 to 45 minutes.

Begin this hike by walking north along the retired doubletrack, past the barrier that blocks it to use by motor vehicles. This route leads generally north under the intermittent shade of a scattered timberline forest of lodgepole and whitebark pines, ascending grassy slopes clothed in sagebrush and splashed with the colors of a variety of wildflowers, including gilia, Indian paintbrush, helenium, cinquefoil, lupine, mariposa tulip, wallflower, aster, dandelion, pussy paws, and pennyroyal. The massive, reddish alpine mountain that dominates the view ahead is 11,462-foot Sonora Peak.

The closed doubletrack, quite steep at times, leads up to the cold runoff of a wildflower-decorated spring, then quickly narrows to singletrack. You will splash through the runoff of another cold spring, this one decorated by elephant heads and shooting stars.

Now ascend steep grassy slopes to the west-trending ridge emanating from Sonora Peak. This ridgetop at 10,400 feet is known as St. Marys Pass. The views that have continually expanded throughout this ascent are even more breathtaking at this point, and are surpassed only by the view from Sonora Peak far above.

The narrow path you have been following continues northward from here toward the reddish cone of Stanislaus Peak. Another faint path branches left from here, eventually leading into the upper Clark Fork of the Stanislaus River.

To your south and southwest, immediately across CA 108, is an area of high volcanic peaks, clearly illustrating the depth of the volcanic flows that buried this region before the Sierra Nevada rose to its present height. In the west, the thickly forested western slope of the Sierra is interrupted by the impressive Dardanelles. In the northwest, volcanic peaks of the Sierra crest stretch away toward the Lake Tahoe region.

You will notice a marked difference in the topography north of Sonora Pass, compared with that south of the pass. To the north the character of the landscape is highly scenic, but is more subdued than the magnificent alpine terrain to the south. Consequently, Sonora Pass is often considered the geographical dividing point between the "High" Sierra and the Northern Sierra.

After absorbing the far-ranging vistas from the pass, backtrack to the trailhead.

14
BLUE CANYON

Highlights: This short but memorable alpine hike leads into a glaciated volcanic canyon where one of the most magnificent floral displays anywhere in California can be seen and enjoyed.

General location: Emigrant Wilderness (Stanislaus National Forest), 45 miles northeast of Sonora, and 1.5 miles southwest of Sonora Pass.

Distance: 3.6 miles.

Elevation gain: 1,020 to 1,280 feet.

Trailhead elevation: 8,720 feet at the lower trailhead, or 8,980 feet at the upper trailhead.

High point: Blue Canyon Lake, 10,000 feet.

Best season: July through early October.

Water availability: Abundant. Treat before drinking, or take your own.

Maps: Stanislaus National Forest map; Emigrant Wilderness map (topographic); USGS Sonora Pass 7.5-minute quad.

Permits: Not required for day hiking.

Key points:
0.0 Trailhead on California Highway 108.
0.3 Trails from upper and lower trailheads join; continue ascending Blue Canyon.
0.9 Cross "east fork" of Blue Canyon's creek.
1.8 Blue Canyon Lake.

Blue Canyon

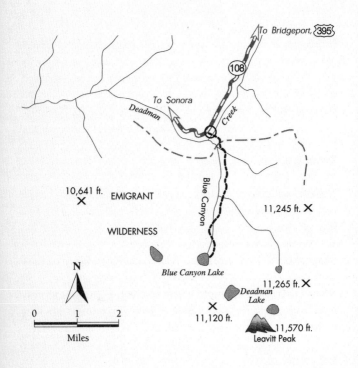

To Bridgeport, 395

108

To Sonora

Deadman

Creek

Blue Canyon

10,641 ft.
✕ EMIGRANT

11,245 ft. ✕

WILDERNESS

N

Blue Canyon Lake

11,265 ft. ✕
Deadman
Lake

0   1   2

✕
11,120 ft.

11,570 ft.
Leavitt Peak

Miles

Finding the trailhead: There is no signed trailhead for Blue Canyon hikers. You must park in one of a few turnouts on California Highway 108. Thus, it is wise to use the Sonora Pass quad and/or the Stanislaus National Forest map to help you identify Blue Canyon so you know when to park.

Just before CA 108 passes the mouth of Blue Canyon, there is parking on the left (northwest) side of the road for about three vehicles. This spot is just above two short switchbacks on the road, and is 2.7 miles southwest of Sonora Pass, and 6.5 miles east of the Kennedy Meadows turnoff. From this point you can see Blue Canyon's creek cascading into Deadman Creek just southeast of the highway, as well as the trail ascending into the canyon.

If this parking area is full, look for the larger parking area 0.2 mile southwest of (below) the upper parking area, 2.9 miles from Sonora Pass, and 6.3 miles east of the Kennedy Meadows turnoff. This parking area lies immediately above (east of) a very sharp bend in the highway.

The hike: Blue Canyon is truly one of the most scenic areas in the entire state. This deeply glaciated canyon, surrounded by striking volcanic peaks and ridges, is a natural flower garden containing a vast collection of colorful wildflowers.

At the head of the canyon, lying under impressive 11,000-foot peaks, are two very beautiful alpine lakes. No fish live in these lakes, but the vivid scenery is adequate compensation for the lack of a trout dinner. Campfires are prohibited above 9,000 feet in the Emigrant Wilderness, which includes all of Blue Canyon.

Starting from the upper parking area on California Highway 108, descend steeply into Deadman Creek. After hopping across this creek, you will pick up a good trail ascending into Blue Canyon just north of its creek.

If you are departing from the lower parking area, however, descend into Deadman Creek and pick up a good path that climbs along the west side of Blue Canyon's creek. Both trails join in Blue Canyon in about 0.3 mile, after avoiding a narrow chasm at the canyon's mouth.

If you started at the upper trailhead, you climb to a lodgepole and whitebark pine-clad bench after crossing Deadman Creek, then enter the Emigrant Wilderness. Follow this sometimes faint path up the canyon toward a pyramidal volcanic peak in the south. The mountains surrounding this canyon are obviously of volcanic origin. This rock was resistant enough that glaciers were able to carve out many deep cirques and excavate basins that contain two alpine lakes. Since most volcanic rocks are much less resistant to glacial attack than granite, lake basins are rarely gouged into a volcanic landscape. The resulting glacially sculpted volcanic peaks in this canyon are stunning.

Tree cover in the canyon is sparse, restricted to its lower end. You pass by scattered stands of whitebark pine in the lower canyon, with a few lodgepole and western white pines on the west-facing slopes above. Whitebark pines will accompany hikers partway up this canyon, often stunted and deformed by years of savage winters.

The variety of wildflowers in this canyon, particularly in the lower half of the canyon, is truly unbelievable, putting forth a dramatic, colorful display, especially in late July through mid-August.

In these natural flower gardens you will find, among a variety of other flowers: red Indian paintbrush, aster, helenium, corn lily, red columbine, green gentian, scarlet gilia, stonecrop, mariposa tulip, monkey flower, larkspur, mule's ears, lupine, wallflower, King's smooth sandwort, yampah, buttercup, phlox, shooting star, whorled penstemon, senecio, whitehead, pennyroyal, mountain sorrel, and alpine pynocoma.

Continuing your leisurely walk amid flower gardens and clumps of stunted whitebark pines, you approach the cascading creek before climbing steeply beside it on the now-gravelly trail. Exercise care along this stretch—walking on volcanic gravel tends to resemble walking on marbles, and a misstep can send you flying.

Above this brief climb you have excellent views of snow-streaked volcanic crags looming boldly at the canyon's head.

Water in Blue Canyon is very abundant, issuing forth from the porous volcanic rock and spilling down steep slopes to feed Blue Canyon's creek.

You will hop across the "east fork" of Blue Canyon's creek, draining Deadman Lake and the permanent snowfields clinging to the flanks of 11,570-foot Leavitt Peak, highest in the Emigrant Wilderness. You can ascend this fine canyon to Deadman Lake, or from Blue Canyon Lake you can hike cross-country to Deadman Lake, then descend via the east fork for a rewarding and highly scenic alpine hike.

Your trail grows faint beyond the east fork, but shortly reappears as an obscure path. Continue south, passing just west of the colorful landmark pyramid that has guided you from the lower canyon, then descend steeply to cross the creek in a narrow gorge. Over-the-shoulder views from this vicinity include the Sierra Nevada crest from Sonora Peak north to Stanislaus Peak. As you proceed up the canyon, notice that the variety of wildflowers has diminished markedly, but color is still fairly abundant.

You eventually end your climb at incomparable Blue Canyon Lake. This small, turquoise lake lies in a deep cirque at 10,000 feet, surrounded by magnificent volcanic crags soaring more than 1,000 feet above its shoreline. The colorful pinnacle just east of the lake is especially striking.

From Blue Canyon Lake, return to the trailhead.

15
COUNTY LINE TRAILHEAD TO THE DARDANELLES

Highlights: This short, scenic hike follows an unmaintained but easy-to-follow trail that traverses below the southeast slopes of the spectacular Dardanelles on the west slope of the Sierra.
General location: Carson-Iceberg Wilderness (Stanislaus National Forest), 37 miles northeast of Sonora.
Distance: 5 miles.
Elevation gain: 500 feet.
Trailhead elevation: 7,200 feet.
High point: 7,700 feet.
Best season: Mid-June through early October.
Water availability: Take your own.
Maps: Stanislaus National Forest map; Carson-Iceberg Wilderness map (topographic); USGS Spicer Meadow Reservoir 7.5-minute quad.
Permits: Not required for day hiking.

Key points:
0.0 County Line Trailhead; proceed straight ahead then turn right (southeast) after 150 yards onto McCormick Creek Trail.
2.5 Junction with faint Dardanelles Spur Trail.

Finding the trailhead: About 17.2 miles west of Sonora Pass on California Highway 108, and about 49 miles east of Sonora, turn north where a sign indicates Clark Fork Road.

County Line Trailhead to the Dardanelles

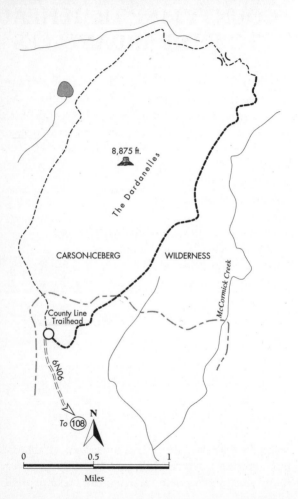

8,875 ft.

The Dardanelles

CARSON-ICEBERG   WILDERNESS

McCormick Creek

County Line
Trailhead

6N09

To 108

N

0   0.5   1
Miles

This paved road, Forest Road 7N83, crosses the Middle Fork, then the Clark Fork Stanislaus River. After driving 0.9 mile from the highway, turn left onto FR 6N06 where a sign indicates Fence Creek Campground. Follow this dusty dirt road west, avoiding the right-branching spur road to Fence Creek Campground after 0.2 mile. After driving 6.4 miles from the highway, avoid right-branching FR 6N06A, and continue another 0.7 mile to the County Line Trailhead at the road's end.

The hike: This scenic hike traverses beneath the intriguing Dardanelles, a striking volcanic formation rising well over 1,000 feet above the surrounding heavily forested landscape. The Dardanelles are part of the lava flows that buried this region millions of years ago. Since much of the volcanic material has been removed by repeated episodes of glaciation, the Dardanelles stand like a volcanic island in a "sea" of granite.

From the trailhead, you pass amid stumps and other scars of past logging, and after 150 yards branch right onto the McCormick Creek Trail, a closed doubletrack, and head northeast through a forest of Jeffrey pine and white fir, obtaining occasional tree-framed views of the Three Chimneys and Castle Rock to the southeast.

After red fir joins the forest, you pass through a small meadow where your route narrows to singletrack, then enter the Carson-Iceberg Wilderness and leave most of the stumps and logging scars behind. From this point, the Dardanelles loom boldly on the northern skyline, their dark volcanic cliffs contrasting with the greenery that thrives in the rich volcanic soil of their lower slopes.

Continuing on a northeasterly course, pass through more small meadows that contain, among the previously mentioned forest trees, lodgepole pine and aspen, before strolling across an aspen-rich meadow. The fantastic castlelike formation rising in the eastern foreground is Peak 9086, lying on the ridge 1 mile southwest of Dardanelles Cone.

Your trail passes through more aspen-clad meadows that host corn lilies, willows, currants, and assorted wildflowers. While crossing these meadows, early-morning and late-afternoon hikers are apt to see some of the abundant mule deer that inhabit this region.

You eventually begin climbing, passing an isolated stand of black cottonwood. Several yards thereafter, you reach the junction with a very faint northbound trail, the Dardanelles Spur Trail. The McCormick Creek Trail continues east.

This junction makes a convenient turnaround point. From there, retrace your steps beneath the towering volcanic ridge of the Dardanelles.

16
GIANELLI TRAILHEAD TO POWELL LAKE

Highlights: This scenic subalpine trip on the west slope of the Central Sierra features broad vistas, visits a delightful timberline lake, and surveys contrasting landscapes of granitic and volcanic rocks.

General location: Emigrant Wilderness (Stanislaus National Forest), 30 miles northeast of Sonora.

Distance: 4.6 miles.

Elevation gain and loss: +500 feet, -150 feet.

Trailhead elevation: 8,560 feet.

High point: 9,161 feet.

Best season: July through early October.

Water availability: Take your own.

Maps: Stanislaus National Forest map; Emigrant Wilderness map (topographic); USGS Cooper Peak, and Pinecrest 7.5-minute quads.

Permits: Not required for day hiking.

Key points:
0.0 Gianelli Trailhead.
1.3 Burst Rock.
2.2 Junction with unsigned northbound trail to Powell Lake; turn left (north).
2.3 Powell Lake.

Gianelli Trailhead to Powell Lake

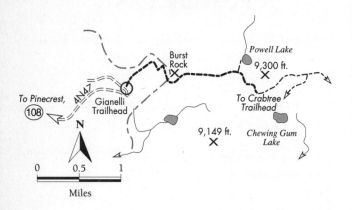

To Pinecrest, 108

Gianelli Trailhead

Burst Rock

Powell Lake
9,300 ft.

To Crabtree Trailhead

9,149 ft.

Chewing Gum Lake

N

0   0.5   1

Miles

Finding the trailhead: Proceed east from Sonora on California Highway 108 for about 30 miles, then turn right (east) onto the paved two-lane road where a sign indicates "Pinecrest— 1." The Summit District ranger station is located on the east side of the highway at this turnoff. After driving 0.4 mile, turn right again and follow signs to Dodge Ridge Ski Area. Turn right once again after another 3 miles; a sign here points to Aspen Meadow, Bell Meadow, and Crabtree Camp. This turn is located just before a large sign declaring the entrance to Dodge Ridge Ski Area.

After turning right here onto Forest Road 4N26, the road leads southwest for 0.4 mile to a stop sign. Turn left (southeast) here and ascend steadily to the junction with the southbound road to Bell Meadow, 1.7 miles from the stop sign and 5.5 miles from the highway. Stay left (east) at the junction and drive through the Aspen Meadow Pack Station complex on the dirt road, beyond which you follow one-lane pavement on a steady ascent.

The pavement ends 1.3 miles beyond the pack station, and the wide dirt road ahead is rough, with washboards and rocky stretches for the remaining distance to Gianelli Trailhead. After driving 1.4 miles from the end of the pavement, stay left (east) where a signed spur road branches right to Crabtree Trailhead. Continue ascending, now on FR 4N47, for another 4.1 miles to the trailhead parking area, 12.3 miles from the highway. Here you will find ample space to park about 15 vehicles, but no signs designating the trailhead parking area.

The hike: Long before the Sierra Nevada was uplifted to its present height, volcanic eruptions from the east flowed over much of the landscape north of Yosemite National Park. These flows buried most of the exposed granitic bedrock in the region. When the glaciers formed, they carried away much of the volcanic debris that buried the landscape, reexposing the granitic bedrock.

Beyond the northern end of the High Sierra, this glacially reexposed granite gives way to deep volcanic deposits that weren't completely removed by glaciation, thus forming a landscape much different than areas farther south in the Sierra. The contrasts between the two rock types is often striking, making this hike not only scenic but also offering insights into the geologic history of the region.

This fine short hike ascends gradually from the trailhead to the panoramic viewpoint of Burst Rock, then drops into a granite bowl where you find lovely Powell Lake.

The rock-lined trail begins at the north end of the parking area and ascends gradually northeast through a shady forest of red fir, mountain hemlock, and western white pine to a granitic ridge, the Stanislaus River–Clavey River divide, where trailside trees filter the northward view across the South Fork Stanislaus River canyon. The trail follows an eastbound course just below the ridge, then turns south at a ridgeline saddle. The trail ahead ascends gently to moderately, making the ascent to Burst Rock far more pleasant than the abruptly rising old trail that hikers used to follow.

The trail ascends through a shady pine, fir, and hemlock forest and among granite slabs to the west shoulder of Burst Rock. There you pass a sign that details the brief history of the Emigrant trail known as the West Walker–Sonora Road, a very difficult route that gave the Emigrant Wilderness its name. From this point onward you enjoy expansive westward views across the heavily forested western Sierra foothills.

The trail ahead gently ascends sandy slopes south of Burst Rock, then gradually descends to an open saddle. Don't miss the short detour to the granite boulders capping Burst Rock, just northwest of the trail. From there, superb vistas unfold, some of the most far-ranging on the entire hike. The view north across the South Fork Stanislaus River, with its glacially reexposed granite, provides a marked contrast with the volcanic peaks rising in odd forms north of the river. These peaks include 9,603-foot Cooper Peak, 9,600-foot Castle Rock, and the Three Chimneys.

Soaring alpine peaks of the Sierra Nevada crest rise to the east, and in the southeast a low, heavily glaciated rocky plateau extends toward the eastern boundary of Yosemite National Park. In the south, thickly forested, gentle westslope terrain contrasts vividly with all the exposed granite lying immediately to the east. These vistas will accompany hikers through most of this ridgetop journey.

A descent of 250 feet through subalpine forest follows east of Burst Rock. At the bottom of this descent, in a saddle fringed with stunted trees and red heather, penstemon, aster, and lupine, you reach the unmarked trail on your left that leads to 8,800-foot Powell Lake.

Turn left onto that trail and follow it north for 0.1 mile to the lake. Boot-worn trails continue around the west and north shores, but on its east shore steep granite plunges into the lake. Bound in a shallow granite bowl, the lake is fringed by meadows and surrounded by an open subalpine forest of mountain hemlock, and lodgepole and western white pines.

A pair of rocky peninsulas jut into the lakes from the north shore. Fishing here is poor, but the beautiful surroundings and fine views north to Cooper Peak and Castle Rock make this a good destination for a day's outing in the Northern Sierra.

From the lake, day hikers eventually backtrack to the trailhead.

17
GREEN CREEK
TO GREEN LAKE

Highlights: This fine day hike follows an east-side canyon toward the Sierra crest, and features memorable vistas of colorful metamorphic peaks, and good fishing amid majestic surroundings at forest-fringed Green Lake.

General location: Hoover Wilderness (Toiyabe National Forest), 10 miles southwest of Bridgeport.

Distance: 4.8 miles.

Elevation gain: 800 feet.

Trailhead elevation: 8,100 feet.

High point: Green Lake, 8,900 feet.

Best season: July through early October.

Water availability: Abundant. Treat before drinking or take your own.

Maps: Toiyabe National Forest map; Hoover Wilderness map (topographic); USGS Dunderberg Peak 7.5-minute quad.

Permits: Not required for day hiking.

Key points:
0.0 Green Creek Trailhead.
1.2 Hoover Wilderness boundary.
2.3 Junction with West Lake Trail; bear right (west).
2.4 Green Lake.

Finding the trailhead: From U.S. Highway 395, 3.8 miles south of the Bridgeport Ranger Station in Bridgeport, and

Green Creek to Green Lake

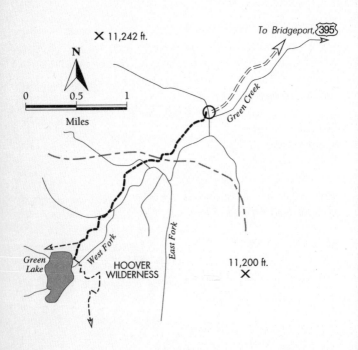

85.75 miles north of Bishop, turn southwest onto the signed Green Creek Road. Bear left after 1 mile where a sign points to Green Creek. After another 2.5 miles, turn right; the Virginia Lakes Road continues straight ahead. Proceed another 5.8 miles to the trailhead at the end of the road.

The hike: Visiting a beautiful subalpine lake, this interesting eastern Sierra day hike surveys a landscape of colorful peaks, differing in color from the "typical" white or gray granite found in most east-side canyons. Featuring a maximum return for a minimum investment of time and effort, the hike should appeal to angler, photographer, and anyone else who enjoys majestic mountain scenery.

The trail begins at the northwest end of the parking area and heads southwest through a forest of lodgepole and Jeffrey pines, aspen, and juniper. Ahead lie the conical alpine peaks encircling the upper West Fork Green Creek and Glines Canyon.

You soon begin negotiating a moderate series of elevation-gaining switchbacks. A pause during this ascent offers over-the-shoulder views down the U-shaped trough of Green Canyon to the Bodie Hills in the eastern distance.

Entering the Hoover Wilderness at a Toiyabe National Forest sign, the trail then edges close to Green Creek, which is dammed here by aspen-gnawing beavers. Continuing up the canyon, you'll notice the East Fork Green Creek opening up to the south, exposing the massive red flanks of Dunderberg Peak, which, at 12,374 feet, is the highest summit in the Green Creek area.

The trail follows the course of the West Fork Green Creek in a forest of aspen and lodgepole pine. In October you are rewarded not only with solitude but also a colorful display of turning aspens. The trail crosses several creeklets issuing from the lower slopes of Monument Ridge, where you are treated to a variety of colorful wildflowers in season.

After 2.3 miles of steady ascent from the trailhead, you reach a junction with the right-branching trail to West Lake. Turn right onto that trail and stroll through the forest for 0.1 mile to the north shore of large, deep Green Lake. The trail follows the north shore for 0.25 mile to the junction with the steep westbound trail leading to West Lake. You can continue on the trail partway around the west shore until the trail begins ascending the precipitous U-shaped trough of Glines Canyon toward Virginia Pass on the Sierra crest.

At the lake you will find that the trout population is abundant and hungry, but even if you forgot to bring your fishing tackle, you will still enjoy the dramatic vistas from the lakeshore. In the northwest, a white ribbon of water falls over a band of red rock on the flanks of Peak 10,900. Glines Canyon, with its willow-clad meadows and sparse timber, sweeps steadily westward from the lake to Virginia Pass, blocked by semipermanent snow and a 200-foot-high headwall.

18
EMMA LAKE

Highlights: This short hike quickly leads to a scenic and seldom-visited timberline lake in the Eastern Sierra, where fishing is productive and vistas are outstanding.
General location: Toiyabe National Forest, 15 miles west-northwest of Bridgeport, and 10 miles southeast of Sonora Pass.
Distance: 2 miles.
Elevation gain: 750 feet.
Trailhead elevation: 8,560 feet.
High point: Emma Lake, 9,300 feet.
Best season: Early July through September.
Water availability: Available at the lake. Treat before drinking, or take your own.
Maps: Toiyabe National Forest map; Hoover Wilderness map (topographic); USGS Fales Hot Springs 7.5-minute quad.
Permits: Not required.

Key points:
0.0 Emma Lake Trailhead
1.0 Emma Lake

Finding the trailhead: From U.S. Highway 395, 15.1 miles northwest of Bridgeport, and 0.7 mile southeast of the US 395/California Highway 108 junction, turn south onto Forest Road 066, signed for Little Walker River and National Forest Campground.

Emma Lake

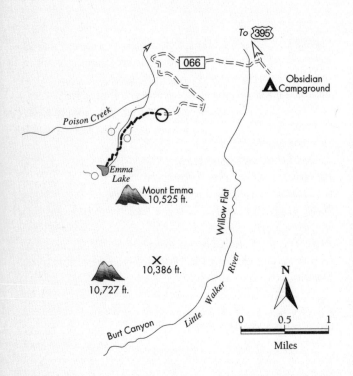

Follow this graded dirt road, which is rocky with washboards, as it ascends south above the meadows of the Little Walker River. After 3.4 miles you cross the bridge spanning Molybdenite Creek and, immediately thereafter, avoid the left-branching spur road leading to Obsidian Campground. After 3.6 miles you pass the signed Burt Canyon Trail and begin a westbound ascent.

As you continue to ascend, the road becomes much rougher and quite rocky, yet remains passable to carefully driven passenger cars. Avoid a right-branching road after 4.5 miles, and a left-branching, southbound doubletrack at 6 miles. You reach the loop at the road's end, 6.7 miles from the highway, where you find a Hoover Wilderness information signboard, and room enough for about eight vehicles. You find several spurs used as undeveloped campsites en route to the trailhead.

The hike: Emma Lake is a seldom-visited timberline gem set in a small cirque beneath broad Mount Emma in the volcanic highlands east of the West Walker River and the Sierra crest. This open country, reminiscent of the Rocky Mountains and recommended by the Forest Service as an addition to the Hoover Wilderness, is delightful hiking country overlooked by most California hikers. This short hike has a few steep grades, but most hikers won't mind as they will reach the lovely timberline lake in less than one hour.

The trail begins as a long-closed logging road, ascending a moderate grade among stumps and a forest of lodgepole and western white pines, and red fir. Fine, over-the-shoulder views framed by trailside trees extend northeast to the towering 11,000-foot peaks of the Sweetwater Mountains.

Quite soon the route narrows to singletrack and within minutes you crest a minor ridge, then follow a brief descent across open slopes into a small bowl, enjoying northward views of the West Walker River canyon along the way. After crossing the dry gully on the floor of the bowl, climb steeply to quickly gain a low rocky ridge (a moraine), fringed by whitebark pine and mountain hemlock. Mount Emma towers above the trail here, and the inviting timberline landscapes of the Emma Lake cirque beckon you onward.

The trail descends off the moraine and enters an open, tree-studded basin draining Emma Lake creek. Sagebrush, snowberry, and fields of mule's ears carpet the nearby volcanic slopes. Upon entering the basin, the tread briefly grows obscure as you head south through a sedge-filled meadow, rich with the yellow blooms of cinquefoil and senecio, and the lavender flowers of aster. Jump across the runoff of the spring shown on the topo map, issuing from a grove of lodgepole pines at the trailside.

The trail inclines once again beyond the meadow, leading out of the timberline forest of whitebark pine and mountain hemlock to Emma Lake's outlet stream. Cross the shallow, multiple branches of the stream just below its emergence from a small, rubbly terminal moraine. The stream's banks host rich greenery, the vivid blue blossoms of larkspur, and the lavender blooms of fireweed.

One final sustained steep grade, moderating in a few places, leads 0.2 mile and 250 feet up past stunted whitebarks and over the corrugated terrain of glacial moraines to the lovely emerald waters of Emma Lake.

Encircled by light gray–colored volcanic ridges feathered on their crests with spreading, multibranched whitebark pines, and with the broad dome of 10,525-foot Mount Emma rising above the southeast shore, this is a beautiful lake lying in a grand Eastern Sierra setting. Large springs issue from the talus slopes south of the lake and sustain its waters throughout the summer, long after snowfields have melted. Scattered groves of whitebark pines and thickets of willow fringe the lake, and an angler's trail encircles it. The lake is lightly used, even on weekends, making it one of the better easy getaways in the Northern Sierra.

You must eventually leave Emma Lake and backtrack to the trailhead.

Saddlebag Lake to Greenstone Lake

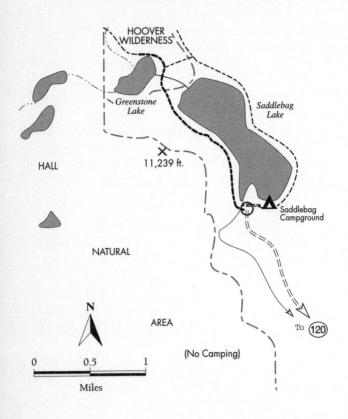

19
SADDLEBAG LAKE TO GREENSTONE LAKE

Highlights: This short trip, above 10,000 feet throughout, tours a beautiful lake-filled basin beneath the granite peaks of the northern Sierra crest.

General location: Hoover Wilderness (Inyo National Forest), 7 miles west of Lee Vining, and 3.5 miles north of Tioga Pass.

Distance: 3.8 miles.

Elevation gain and loss: +150 feet, -160 feet.

Trailhead elevation and High point: 10,150 feet.

Best season: Mid-July through September.

Water availability: Abundant. Treat before drinking, or take your own.

Maps: Hoover Wilderness map (topographic); USGS Yosemite National Park map; USGS Tioga Pass 7.5-minute quad.

Permits: Not required for day hiking.

Key points:

0.0 Saddlebag Lake Trailhead.

1.6 Junction with trail from boat dock; turn left (west) toward Greenstone Lake.

1.9 North shore of Greenstone Lake.

Finding the trailhead: Follow California Highway 120 either 2.1 miles northeast from Tioga Pass, or 10 miles west from

U.S. Highway 395 to the signed turnoff to Saddlebag Lake. Follow the narrow and rough dirt road for 2.4 miles to the signed trailhead parking area south of the lake.

If you choose to ride the boat to the head of the lake or back to the trailhead, rather than hike the shoreline trail, continue up the road for another 0.2 mile to the parking lot at the Saddlebag Lake store, and make arrangements for the boat ride and for the pick-up time for the return trip.

The hike: This short, lofty excursion is an immensely rewarding trek, following the shore of sprawling Saddlebag Lake en route to one of more than one dozen alpine lakes spread out across the headwaters basins of Lee Vining and Mill creeks. The trail is gentle enough for any hiker to enjoy, though the high elevations, combined with the dramatic scenery, are likely to leave most people breathless.

You have three options for returning to the trailhead from Greenstone Lake: (1) retrace your inbound steps; (2) follow the old mining road around the northeast shore of the lake for 2 miles; or if you make arrangements at the Saddlebag Lake store, (3) ride the boat back to the trailhead.

From the trailhead parking area, cross Saddlebag Lake Road and follow an old road downhill to Lee Vining Creek below the lake's dam. From here, the road quickly climbs to the dam where the trail begins. Already above timberline, the trail undulates above the lake's west shore over the crunchy red and gray metamorphic rocks that dominate the landscape east of the Sierra crest. Only a scattering of krummholz whitebark pines dot the trailside slopes, while red heather, a common alpine plant in the Sierra, is the most prevalent wildflower seen en route.

About midway around the lake, the granite crags of the Sierra crest come into view, contrasting in color and in character with the metamorphic peaks and ridges nearby. It is obvious why John Muir so aptly named the Sierra Nevada the "Range of Light," because the nearly white peaks along the crest not only reflect the intense alpine sunshine but also almost seem to radiate a light of their own.

As you approach the head of Saddlebag Lake, the pointed summit of 12,242-foot North Peak and its permanent snowfield come into view on the western skyline. After 1.5 miles, the trail fades into obscurity in an alpine meadow above and west of Saddlebag Lake. However, cairns lead you the short distance to the meandering creek emanating from nearby Greenstone Lake, where a search for a log crossing helps you to avoid wet feet.

Once beyond the creek you will soon intersect a trail leading west to the shoreline of Greenstone Lake, one of many alpine gems in the 20 Lakes Basin. Turn left onto that trail and proceed to the lake's north shore where the trail and the old mining road, 0.3 mile from Saddlebag Lake's upper boat dock, nearly coalesce.

Set beneath the towering crag of 12,590-foot Mount Conness, presently visible to the southwest, and the bold pyramid of 12,242-foot North Peak, Greenstone Lake provides perhaps the most dramatic scene of alpine grandeur in the Saddlebag Lake area. Stunted groves of whitebark and lodgepole pines stud the ice-polished granite surrounding this beautiful lake.

Eventually you must return to the trailhead from Green-stone Lake, following one of the three return options mentioned above.

20
SADDLEBAG LAKE ROAD
TO GARDISKY LAKE

Highlights: This short but rigorous hike quickly leads hikers to a pristine timberline lake, and dramatic views of the Sierra crest, and the northern peaks of Yosemite National Park.
General location: Inyo National Forest, 3 miles north of Tioga Pass.
Distance: 2 miles.
Elevation gain: 750 feet.
Trailhead elevation: 9,750 feet.
High point: Gardisky Lake, 10,500 feet.
Best season: Mid-July through September.
Water availability: Available en route and at the lake. Treat before drinking, or take your own.
Maps: Inyo National Forest map; USGS Mount Dana, and Tioga Pass 7.5-minute quads.
Permits: Not required.

Key points:
0.0 Gardisky Lake Trailhead.
1.0 Gardisky Lake.

Finding the trailhead: Follow California Highway 120 to the signed turnoff to Saddlebag Lake, 2.1 miles northeast of Tioga Pass, and 10 miles west of U.S. Highway 395 at Lee Vining. Proceed north on Saddlebag Lake Road, which is

Saddlebag Lake Road to Gardisky Lake

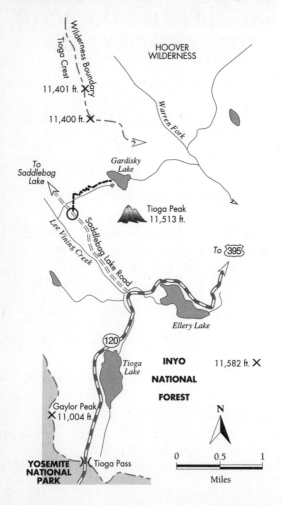

Tioga Crest

Wilderness Boundary

HOOVER
WILDERNESS

11,401 ft. ✕

11,400 ft. ✕

Warren Fork

To
Saddlebag
Lake

Gardisky
Lake

Lee Vining Creek

Saddlebag Lake Road

Tioga Peak
11,513 ft.

To 395

Ellery Lake

120

Tioga
Lake

INYO

11,582 ft. ✕

NATIONAL

Gaylor Peak
✕ 11,004 ft.

FOREST

N

YOSEMITE
NATIONAL
PARK

Tioga Pass

0   0.5   1

Miles

rough with rocks and washboards, for 1.2 miles to the signed Gardisky Lake Trailhead, located on the left (west) side of the road. There is room enough for eight vehicles at the trailhead, where you will find an information signboard, map, and trailhead register.

The hike: Gardisky Lake is an alpine gem, straddling the Tioga Crest above Saddlebag Lake, and though the hike to its shores is short, it is steep enough in places to give hikers a feeling of accomplishment. Grand alpine scenery and 30-minute access to a lovely alpine basin combine to make this trip one of the best short hikes in the Northern Sierra.

The trail begins with a deceptively gentle grade from the east side of Saddlebag Lake Road, heading northeast into grass-carpeted lodgepole pine forest. The trail angles uphill, and you work your way upward at a steep grade beneath a canopy of lodgepoles, to a crossing of a small cascading stream. The trail continues to ascend very steeply over varicolored metamorphic rocks above the north banks of the tumbling, willow-bordered stream through the gradually thinning lodgepole forest.

Glorious views open as you ascend, stretching past the towering cone of Mount Dana to the Kuna Crest in the south, and westward across upper Lee Vining Creek to the gleaming white granite of the Sierra crest, punctuated by 12,000-foot White Mountain, 12,590-foot Mount Conness, and the sheer east face of 12,242-foot North Peak.

As the lodgepoles diminish in numbers, spreading whitebark pines, along with a scattering of gnarled Sierra junipers, begin to dominate the forest scheme. After ascending about 700 short but breathtaking feet, the grade moderates when you open up into a lovely timberline meadow fringed by stunted whitebarks. The trail then rises gently up to a broad, 10,500-foot saddle, where the tread disappears in the turf. A pair of beautiful tarns lie just ahead, and by staying to their left (north) you will reach Gardisky Lake within a few hundred yards.

This fine timberline basin shows virtually no signs of human impact, which is surprising considering its short distance from the trailhead. All hikers must do their utmost to leave no trace of their passing while at Gardisky Lake to help preserve its pristine qualities.

The basin surrounding the lake is exceptionally beautiful, surrounded by turf, meadows, and picturesque stands of stunted whitebark pines. The red alpine summit of 11,513-foot Tioga Peak rises immediately south of the lake and its rubbly slopes can be scaled for boundless vistas via a Class 2 scramble up the northwest ridge. The lake drains eastward into the Warren Fork of Lee Vining Creek, but like so many lakes in this part of the Sierra, it straddles the crest of a high divide.

After enjoying the Gardisky Lake basin, you eventually stroll back down the short trail to the trailhead.

For More Information

For additional information regarding these hikes in the Northern Sierra Nevada, updated information on backcountry conditions, and information regarding wilderness permits and permit reservations, don't hesitate to contact the following agencies.

Hike 1: Quincy Ranger District, 39696 Highway 70, Quincy, CA 95971-9607; 530-283-0555.

Hikes 2, 3, 4, and 5: Beckwourth Ranger District, Mohawk Ranger Station, Mohawk Road, P.O. Box 7, Blairsden, CA 96103; 530-836-2575.

Hike 6: Plumas National Forest, La Porte Ranger District, Challenge Ranger Station, 10087 La Porte Road, P.O. Drawer 369, Challenge, CA 95926; 530-675-2462.

Hike 7: Tahoe National Forest, Nevada City Ranger District, 631 Coyote Street, P.O. Box 6003, Nevada City, CA 95959-6003; 530-265-4531.

Hike 8: Tahoe National Forest, Truckee Ranger District, 10342 Highway 89 North, Truckee, CA 96161; 530-587-3558.

Hike 9: Eldorado National Forest, Amador Ranger District, 26820 Silver Drive, Pioneer, CA 95666; 209-295-4251; or

Eldorado National Forest Information Center, 3070 Camino Heights Drive, Camino, CA 95709; 530-644-6048.

Hikes 9 and 10: Lake Tahoe Basin Management Unit, 870 Emerald Bay Road, Suite 1, South Lake Tahoe, CA 96150; 530-573-2669.

Hike 11: Toiyabe National Forest, Carson Ranger District, 1536 South Carson Street, Carson City, NV 89701; 775-882-2766.

Hikes 13, 14, 15, and 16: Stanislaus National Forest, Summit Ranger District, 1 Pinecrest Lake Road, Pinecrest, CA 95364; 209-965-3434.

Hikes 12, 17, and 18: Toiyabe National Forest, Bridgeport Ranger District, P.O. Box 595, Bridgeport, CA 93517; 760-932-7070.

Hikes 19 and 20: Inyo National Forest, Mono Lake Scenic Area Visitor Center, P.O. Box 130, Lee Vining, CA 93541; 760-647-6629 or (760) 647-6595.

For road conditions and highway information, call CalTrans 24-hour information number for Northern California: 800-427-7623.

About the Author

Ron Adkison, an avid hiker and backpacker, began his outdoor explorations at age six. After more than 30 years of hiking, he has logged more than 8,500 trail miles in ten Western states. He has walked every trail in this guide to provide accurate, firsthand information about the trails, as well as features of ecological and historical interest. When he's not on the trail, Ron lives on his family's mountain ranch in southwest Montana, and with the help of his wife, Lynette, and two children, Ben and Abbey, raises sheep and llamas.

Ron shares his love and enthusiasm for wild places in this, his eleventh guidebook.

Other FalconGuides by Ron Adkison: *Hiking Northern California, Hiking Grand Canyon National Park, Hiking Washington, Hiking Wyoming's Wind River Range, Hiking Grand Staircase–Escalante and the Glen Canyon Region, Best Easy Day Hikes Grand Canyon, Best Easy Day Hikes Grand Staircase–Escalante and the Glen Canyon Region.*

FALCON GUIDES® Leading the Way™

PADDLING GUIDES

Floater's Guide to Colorado
Paddling Minnesota
Paddling Montana
Paddling Okefenokee
Paddling Oregon
Paddling Yellowstone/Grand Teton

ROCK CLIMBING GUIDES

Rock Climbing Arizona
Rock Climbing Colorado
Rock Climbing Montana
Rock Climbing New Mexico & Texas
Rock Climbing Utah
Rock Climbing Washington

ROCKHOUNDING GUIDES

Rockhounding Arizona
Rockhounding California
Rockhounding Colorado
Rockhounding Montana
Rockhounding Nevada
Rockhound's Guide to New Mexico
Rockhounding Texas
Rockhounding Utah
Rockhounding Wyoming

FISHING GUIDES

Fishing Alaska
Fishing the Beartooths
Fishing Florida
Fishing Glacier National Park
Fishing Maine
Fishing Montana
Fishing Wyoming
Fishing Yellowstone
Trout Unlimited's Guide to America's
    100 Best Trout Streams

BIRDING GUIDES

Birding Illinois
Birding Minnesota
Birding Montana
Birding Northern California
Birding Texas
Birding Utah

FIELD GUIDES

Bitterroot: Montana State Flower
Canyon Country Wildflowers
Central Rocky Mountains Wildflowers
Great Lakes Berry Book
New England Berry Book
Ozark Wildflowers
Pacific Northwest Berry Book
Plants of Arizona
Rare Plants of Colorado
Rocky Mountain Berry Book
Scats & Tracks of the Pacific Coast States
Scats & Tracks of the Rocky Mountains
Southern Rocky Mountain Wildflowers
Tallgrass Prairie Wildflowers
Western Trees
Wildflowers of Southwestern Utah
Willow Bark and Rosehips

WALKING

Walking Colorado Springs
Walking Denver
Walking Portland
Walking San Francisco
Walking St. Louis
Walking Virginia Beach

To order check with you local bookseller or
call FALCON® at **1-800-582-2665**.
www.FalconOutdoors.com

 FALCON®

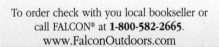